The Millionaire Mindset is a Conditioned Reflex teaches you how to achieve success effortlessly using the psychological method of operant conditioning and the redefined law of attraction.

A successful entrepreneur with multiple advanced degrees in neurology and psychology, Dr. Carlos Garcia-Carranza is married with three children and lives in Florida. Dr. Garcia-Carranza clearly explains the misconceptions and mystical nature of the law of attraction and provides us with a clear, succinct, twenty-first-century scientific explanation of how the law of attraction works and how most successful individuals put it into practice in their daily lives.

Inspired by Rhonda Byrne's *The Secret* and the catastrophic financial condition of 98 percent of the population in this country, Dr. Garcia-Carranza directs his attention to how society indirectly conditions individuals to failure and provides clear methods to reverse the conditioning and produce success using internal methods of operant conditioning in conjunction with the a redefined law of attraction.

Dr. Carlos Garcia-Carranza has an impressive background. He has been involved in a multitude of successful businesses ranging from music production, medicine, psychology, neuropsychology, rehabilitation clinics, pain management clinics, business consulting, asset protection, and real estate.

THE MILLIONAIRE MINDSET
IS A CONDITIONED REFLEX

DR. CARLOS GARCIA-CARRANZA, PsyD

iUniverse, Inc.
New York   Bloomington

The Millionaire Mindset
Is a Conditioned Reflex

iUniverse books may be ordered through booksellers or by contacting:

iUniverse
1663 Liberty Drive
Bloomington, IN 47403
www.iuniverse.com
1-800-Authors (1-800-288-4677)

ISBN: 978-1-4502-2828-2 (sc)
ISBN: 978-1-4502-2829-9 (dj)
ISBN: 978-1-4502-2858-9 (ebook)

Printed in the United States of America

iUniverse rev. date: 04/22/2010

Contents

Chapter 4: The Biology of Belief

Chapter 5: Make Success an Addiction

Chapter 6: The Instructions

Acknowledgements

I want to give my deepest appreciation and gratitude to physicists William Tiller, PhD, Amit Goswami, PhD, John Hagelin, PhD, Fred Alan Wolf, PhD, and Dr. David Albert; to physicians Stuart Hameroff, MD, Jeffrey Satinover, MD, and Andrew B. Newberg, MD; to Dr. Masaru Emoto, Dr. Daniel Monti, and Dr. Joseph Dispenza; and to molecular biologist Dr. Candace Pert. Thanks go also to spiritual teachers, mystics, and scholars: Ramtha, Miceal Ledwith, PhD, Rhonda Byrne, Rusty G. Parrish, John Assaraf, Dr. Rev. Michael Beckwith, Dr. John Demartini, Bob Proctor, Jack Canfield, James Arthur Ray, Dr. Joe Vitale, Lisa Nichols, Marie Diamonds, Dr. John Gray, Esther Hicks, Jerry Hicks, Mike Dooley, Bob Doyle, David Schirmer, Marci Shimoff, Lee Brower, Hale Dwoskin, Cathy Goodman, Morris E. Goodman, Bill Harris, Dr. Ben Johnson, Denis Waitley, and Neale Donald Walsch.

This book would not have been possible without their contribution toward making this world a better place for all. The thoughts, ideas, explanations, and views of this large group of highly dedicated and educated individuals inspired me to conduct my research in neurobiological behavioral conditioning and to formulate a clear and simplistic explanation to clarify the controversial issues that have surrounded the law of attraction for decades.

Introduction

I started writing this book one Sunday afternoon after coming home from church, where Pastor Darrell Owens had spoken about the critical financial situation around the country. This inspired me to look up government statistics. I spent hours reviewing the shocking truth. The information was actually much worse than I'd expected. I was aware of the severity of the overall economic condition of the country but I was completely unaware of the critical financial condition of the individual average American. I started with the idea to write an article for the local newspaper until I realize I had to find a way to reach a much larger audience. I thought about asking to appear on *The Cristina Show* (a very popular *Oprah*-style talk show in the Latin community) since I had been on her show numerous times in the past as an expert in the field of psychology. However, since that would only target the Latin community, I decided the best vehicle for sharing my message would be a book. I sat in front of the computer for days, not knowing where to start. In my briefcase, I had a movie called *The Secret* a friend had given me to watch. I watched the movie three times in a row and pondered my new sense of insight. I started writing with two questions in mind: What is wrong? And what is the solution? Could I help people turn the concepts of *The Secret* into a lifestyle geared toward success?

I have always been interested in educating others, and a large part of my success is directly related to the satisfaction I get from sharing my knowledge with anyone who is willing to listen. The quality and value of any educational information you read always depends on the person who writes it. So, it is important for your evaluation and application of this material to know a little bit about me. I will therefore attempt to give you in a couple of short paragraphs a condensed version of my life's work.

I am a neuropsychologist and, prior to getting my graduate degree at the University of Miami, I worked for several years in the psychiatric unit of one of the nation's top twenty-five hospitals. After graduate school and my medical internship, I began working in the field of drug and food addiction. The field of addiction was one of the most difficult areas in medicine because at that time, research into neurological biochemical processes was in its infancy. Today, research has advanced immensely, and we are much more scientifically informed on neurobiological functions and neurological biochemistry. However, even with the scientific advances in medical methods of addiction treatment, the problem of addiction continues to baffle medical science.

The knowledge I am going to share with you has come to me through many years of experience in this field and various other professional disciplines. I am what most individuals would label an overachiever. I have owned multiple successful businesses, including a psychology office, a medical office, a pain clinic, and a rehabilitation center with programs to retrain stroke patients and regain mobility. I have made substantial financial gains in the stock market and foreign exchange currency markets.

I combined my knowledge of psychology and my interest in finance in order to become a business consultant for one of the largest corporations in the country, analyzing small- to medium-sized businesses in order to increase profit margins. I owned an asset protection and tax avoidance company, a real estate company, and a mortgage company; all of this was achieved in the better part of forty years.

I am not any more special or smarter than any of you. I experienced the same difficulty everyone has passing calculus, physics, organic chemistry, and biochemistry. What makes me somewhat different from other folks is the way I have conditioned myself to think and how I use my hypothalamus—a gland about the size of a golf ball that sits in the middle of the brain. This has allowed me phenomenal success in my life, and the same strategy can work for you.

By simple **operant conditioning** (a term I will explain in depth in this book), I have become a success junkie. I have trained that gland to work overtime in the production of neurological **peptide amino acid** chains, a process I will thoroughly explain so that everyone, without exception, can learn and duplicate the results. I am addicted to success. My mind does not stop; I am always thinking of things I can do and projects I can undertake to take me to the next level. Just like the addict looking for the next fix, I am always on overdrive: reading, searching, and probing for the next achievement. My mind is like radar, constantly analyzing and looking for opportunities. This is a process that comes to me automatically without any effort. As a result, my life is filled with one accomplishment after another.

The key to my success is my addiction to it, which can be explained by the **law of attraction** and the neurological biochemical process of operant conditioning. Accomplishing short- and long-term goals is simple; and can be explained in three simple words—thoughts become things—through a simple process of behavioral operant conditioning.

Some of these terms might be new to you. For your reference, terms that appear in **bold** also appear in the glossary.

At times, the material in this book may seem repetitive. Repetition is a key tenet of learning, especially when your initial goal is to establish a mindset of success. If you come across an idea that sounds familiar or that you know you've already encountered, view that as your opportunity to really focus on the material, absorbing it more deeply into your consciousness.

After decades of success, I am confident in my approach and ready to share it with you. If you're ready to listen, it's time to get started.

CHAPTER 1
The Problem

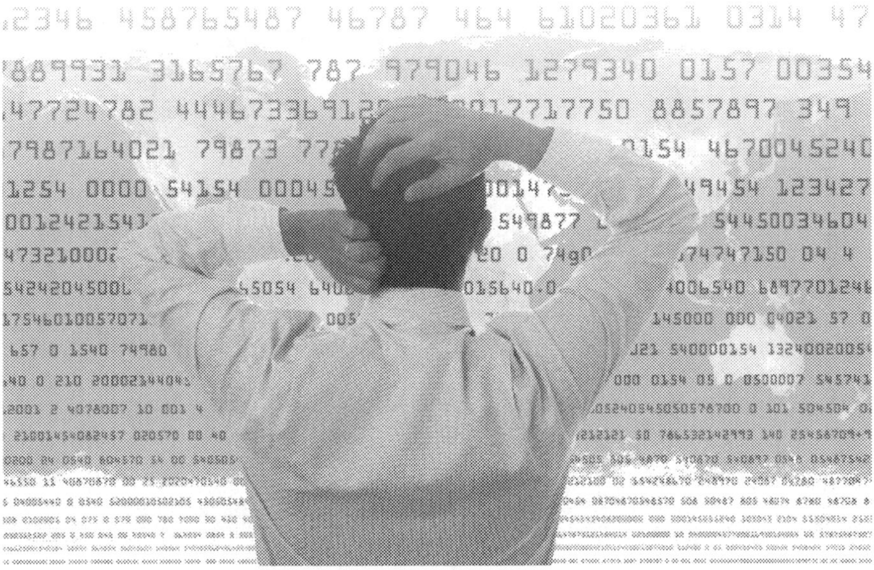

1.1 Do You Live Next to a Millionaire or a Pauper?

We all have that neighbor: the one with the gleaming new cars and the stylishly decorated home. She rolls out of the driveway every morning wearing designer clothing and sunglasses that cost more than your car payment; he can be seen through his living-room window, kicking back on his expensive leather sofa and watching his enormous television. They show up at neighborhood block parties and flash matching white smiles as they boast about having excellent credit and make rueful jokes about giving their twenty-plus credit cards a workout at the mall.

These people are the Joneses, and when the rest of us aren't hating them, we're wishing we were them. Have you ever eyed a neighbor's tailored suit or pricey handbag and felt frustrated that you could not emulate his or her success? How often have you felt that pang of jealousy when Mr. Jones invites you to check out his new boat or Mrs. Jones shows off the diamond bracelet she got for Christmas? When you're struggling to make ends meet, it can be hard not to become bitter at the Joneses' financial success.

I have a secret for you: More than likely, the Joneses are faking every minute of it. If you looked closer at these people, you might see that the Joneses are unhappy individuals constantly worried about their financial wealth and future. In fact, if you looked closer, your envy would surely be replaced with pity.

In most cases, their success process is full of faulty and defective economic strategies combined with an elaborate front to impress others. They use the money from one card to pay for the other. They are always willing to share their faulty methods and techniques with anyone who lends an ear. In the past, this may have seemed smug or condescending to you, but in truth, such advice is a great example of misery loving company. If you adopt any of their financial strategies, this just gives the Joneses one more reason to tell themselves the lie that what they are doing isn't harming their financial future.

Do not let any of these individuals impress or fool you; there is an enormous difference between *financial experts*, who have conditioned themselves to be successful by applying the law of attraction (which will be explained in more detail throughout this book) in their daily lives, and so-called *financial magicians* like the Joneses, who have mastered the art of masking financial catastrophe with a facade of success.

So what's the real secret of living successfully and avoiding piles of debt? Instead of keeping up with the Joneses, how can you learn to ignore the Joneses and forge your own path to financial prosperity?

This book is dedicated to answering that question in depth. But in a nutshell, to enjoy true, constant, ongoing financial success (rather than the temporary flash of bling and glitter you've spotted at the house next door), you need to condition your mind by creating a specific set of thoughts that will generate the same repetitive results. This training of your mind is more commonly known in psychology as *operant conditioning*. This is the psychological behavioral application most widely used to produce changes in behavior. Learning this application in combination with the universal law of attraction will guarantee major life-changing behavioral corrections.

If you haven't heard of operant conditioning or the law of attraction before, don't worry; this book will provide all the education you need. Both of these concepts will be explained in detail. Once you have studied the law of attraction in depth, Chapter 6 will teach you how to use conditioning to apply it to your own life.

Once you learn to harness the power of behavioral conditioning, you will experience real financial success. As your income increases, your savings grow, and you become more and more financially secure, the joy and inspiration you feel will turn even more of your thoughts into reality. Rather than wasting your time showing off purchases you can't afford or envying an indebted lifestyle that will bring more stress than happiness, you can enjoy the confidence of true financial security.

Forget the Joneses. What have truly successful individuals been doing to get where they are? They have been applying this type of operant conditioning on an ongoing basis in their daily lives, and so can you.

1.2 An Ignored Majority

If you're wondering why you've never heard of any of this before, I can tell you the answer: Up until now, unless you have been making more than $250,000 a year, no one has bothered to talk to you.

I have read all of the current top motivational books for the so-called average **entrepreneur**. They all have one thing in common; they target a very small percentage of the population. In fact, there is nothing average about their intended audience at all. The IRS reports that only 2 percent of the households in the United States will report an adjusted gross income of more than $250,000 for the year. Yet, most motivational books are coaching the relatively wealthy. What good does that do the average person?

Many Americans do not have enough money at the end of the month to cover their bills; many are behind in their house payments or are facing **foreclosure**. Maybe you fit this description; maybe you are thinking about **bankruptcy** or living from paycheck to paycheck. Maybe you can't afford a vacation; maybe you have less than $5,000 in your savings account. If any such financial troubles have plagued you, you need to learn your way out of this situation. This entire book will teach, educate, and provide you with a solution to your situation; it is your ticket out of the 98 percent group.

Clearly, it's time for the remaining 98 percent of the population to start figuring out what the other 2 percent is doing right. Ask yourself this question: What secret does this 2 percent group have that the 98 percent majority does not know? The answer is straightforward: As painful as it may sound, the majority of the population has been conditioned to a false belief of success since birth—by school, by parents, by the media, and by design. By default, that group has been conditioned to live in mediocrity and accept failure.

What can be done to help that 98 percent? What would the top financial experts tell you in their motivational books, if they were writing for the average individual?

I will be the first one to tell you I do not have all the answers, but what I do know is that statistics do not lie. All the evidence points in one direction: operant conditioning is both the culprit and the solution. Just like failure, success is a learned behavioral process; it does not happen by accident and certainly has nothing to do with luck. Success is a **conditioned belief**. (Chapter 5 discusses conditioning in more detail.)

You may not want to be one of the Joneses, but you don't want to be a plain old average Joe, either. If you are not in the 2 percent of the population, you are doing something wrong.

I have spent a considerable amount time and effort analyzing individuals in that elite 2 percent group. Very few of these individuals are more special, talented, or intelligent than you. In fact, a large percentage of them lack college diplomas.

If, in the past, you have been discouraged by the idea that you must have an IQ of 180 and a dizzyingly complicated master plan in order to find financial success, I am here to tell you that success can be as simple as realizing your coffee cup is too hot for your hand.

Don't believe me? Just ask Jay Sorenson, who invented the insulated cardboard sleeve that now protects customers from burning themselves on their hot coffee cups. For him, success was as simple as dropping a too-hot cup of coffee in his lap. No one is suggesting that success came easily to him—he started out selling the product out of the back of his car—but it wasn't complicated. Your success does not have to be complicated either, as long as you are willing to apply the concepts in this book.

Whether they've invented a piece of cardboard or programmed a highly complex piece of computer software, all successful individuals, without exception, have only one thing in common: the application of learned behaviors that equip them for success. Anyone can learn these behaviors—including you.

1.3 Where Are the Instructions?

When was the last time someone sat down with you to show you how to make a million dollars? The bookstores are overflowing with books selling the dream. I have found some of these books highly motivational in nature, but at the same time, something was missing: concrete, step-by-step instructions. Sure, it's helpful to hear that I am as capable of financial success as anyone. Sure, we all appreciate knowing that prosperity is within our reach. Still, how can we be expected to reach our financial destination without specific, turn-by-turn directions?

When I was halfway through the manuscript, my publishers asked me if I was writing for commercial success. I guess what they meant to ask was whether I was looking for fame and money. This made me aware that commercial success is largely dependent on the style of writing the writer chooses. Some authors write to pleasure a reader, and some write to educate a reader. If you write with the intention to make millions, you can pick a commercially appealing topic that allows readers to fantasize about their dream lives, and then cleverly disguise it as educational material. The result can be a highly entertaining book occupying another space in the bookshelves with its offerings of unattainable, fantastical goals that, in the end, will leave readers no better off.

This book strives to offer the best of both worlds: pleasurable reading and genuine educational value.

1.4 Why This Book Is Unique

What book has sold thirty million copies and made $748,500,000?

Let me repeat that question: What book has made the truly astronomical sum of seven hundred forty-eight million, five hundred thousand dollars?

The answer is *Think and Grow Rich* by Napoleon Hill, first published in 1937—and that is only one motivational book; there are literally thousands more. How is it possible that this and so many other motivational books have become so popular, and yet the average American is in financial and personal distress? Judging from all the books we've bought, by now we should be millionaires, expert cooks, Olympic-level athletes, feng shui masters, and bountiful gardeners, to name just a few of our talents.

Even after one of the most popular financial books was published to great demand, 98 percent of us remained in the dark. Why?

Obviously, you don't need these books to tell you that you have the potential to reach your dreams; you need to be told how to get there. You need not just generalized encouragement, but a detailed **blueprint** of how to accomplish your financial goals.

1.5 What Is Your Destination?

This book claims to offer you a roadmap—but to where? As you learn new behaviors and explore ways to maximize your financial potential, you will be working toward a successful entrepreneurship in which you personally become the master of your financial destiny.

An **entrepreneur** is a person who has possession of an enterprise, or venture, and assumes significant accountability for the inherent risks and the outcome. Not every entrepreneur is financially successful; plenty of unsuccessful ones can be found in the 98 percent group. But becoming a successful entrepreneur requires no special skills.

A successful entrepreneur is an ambitious leader who combines land, labor, and capital, often to create and market new goods or services. Some well-known examples of entrepreneurs include Craig Jerabeck, Jeb Tyler, and Jason Guck—the founders of 5linx, one of the fastest-growing telecommunication companies for four consecutive years (as ranked in the *Inc. 500*). These three entrepreneurs have achieved a strong position in the fast-growing multibillion-dollar industry of VoIP, or Voice over Internet Protocol. These three visionaries will revolutionize the telecommunication industry; their combined efforts embody the true description of entrepreneurship. All three entrepreneurs not only embrace the millionaire mindset of using behavioral operant conditioning to harness the power of the law of attraction, but they also use this mindset to create new entrepreneurs at their 5linx University.

Understanding this material and taking responsibility to learn its application makes you an entrepreneur by definition. As for becoming a successful entrepreneur ... well, this book is here to help you do just that.

1.6 What Is Wrong with This Country?

What are the odds that, by the age of sixty-five, you will find yourself financially dependent on Social Security, friends, relatives, or charity? The statistics reveal that this outcome is much more likely than you might think. Take a look.

Using a highlighting marker, highlight each of these statistics and concentrate on their truth. These are facts that most of society prefers to ignore. Equip yourself with motivating knowledge as your highlighting ensures that you take the time to truly absorb each statistic:

Out of one hundred people who start working at the age of twenty-five, by the age sixty-five:

- 1 is wealthy.
- 4 have adequate capital stowed away for retirement.
- 3 are still working.
- 63 are dependent on Social Security, friends, relatives or charity.
- 29 are dead.

More Statistics on the "Golden Years" **(courtesy of the Internal Revenue Service):**

- The average savings of a fifty-year-old in the United States is $2500.
- Thirty-two million Americans are currently threatened with bankruptcy.
- More than one million filed for bankruptcy in the year 2000.

More Statistics:
Out of every one hundred people who reach the retirement age of sixty-five:

- 62 retire with less than $25,000 in assets and depend on Social Security or family for their retirements.
- Another 35 retire with less than $100,000 in assets, have some form of pension in addition to Social Security, and are just making it in their retirement. If either Social Security or their pensions went away, they would have a very difficult time surviving.
- 2 of the 3 remaining retirees have adequate pensions or retirement accounts. They have assets of between $100,000 and $750,000. They do appreciate having the additional money they receive from Social Security, but could survive without it.
- The last of these one hundred retirees is the only one who is financially independent. This retiree has assets approaching or exceeding $1,000,000 and does not need the income from Social Security at all.

Which of the above groups will you be in when it is time for you to retire?

Still More Statistics:
According to recent Governmental statistics, most individuals are very concerned about their financial security in retirement. Over 70 percent believe they will not have enough money put away for retirement. Of those between the ages of thirty and fifty-four, almost 80 percent feel this way about their future.

One of the factors is the uncertainty of Social Security and Medicare. In the mid-1970s, two-thirds of the individuals surveyed said they were quite confident Social Security would be there for them when they retired, but the trustees of Social Security and Medicare now estimate that the Social Security fund will be exhausted by 2037 while the Medicare trust fund will be depleted by 2018, slightly sooner than previously forecast. The report also estimates, as it did last year, that by 2017, Social Security will no longer be taking in enough payroll tax to pay all promised benefits and will need to tap the special-issue bonds that make up its trust fund. In order to repay these bonds, the federal government will have to borrow more money, raise taxes, cut spending elsewhere, or reduce benefits.[1]

In 1980, of those surveyed, two-thirds commented that they were not confident that Social Security would be there to support them in retirement. They felt that if Social Security were still a functioning service, it probably would not be paying an adequate amount to cover a reasonable standard of living. A major strategy of the government's Greenspan Commission was to develop a large surplus in the Social Security trust funds from 1990 to about 2010, to cover and help finance the retirement of the huge baby boom generation starting after 2010.[2] What is alarming is that the latest government projections show the expected surplus is shrinking into relative insignificance and the so-called Social Security trust funds are estimated not to have financial reserves that can assure the future payment program to the promised benefits.[3] Repeated financial crises will continue to plague the Social Security system. The Social Security trust funds are full of faulty financial calculations that cannot assure future financial security. The young workers of today will never receive the benefits currently promised to them by the program.

So if this is the case, why aren't individuals storing away hoards of money so they are not part of the statistics? Well, it seems that saving for retirement is a difficult task to master for the average person. Some have difficulty saving on a systematic basis. With others, it is often the case of having good intentions but very poor follow-through. Still others make poor selections with the savings and investment vehicles they choose.

Clearly, the working-class scenario of working and building someone else's empire for forty years while trying to accumulate enough money to retire comfortably does not work. Most people would like to retire with dignity—wouldn't you?

Have I shown you enough? Well, here are a few more facts:

The general picture of prosperity is a thing of the past. With the decline in the stock market and decreasing property values, the brutal fact is that for many baby boomers who are now turning fifty, retirement may not be a pretty picture.

Over the next twenty years, seventy-six million of us born between 1946 and 1964 will hit fifty. For most, that means facing up to the harsh questions of how, or even if, they will be able to afford to retire.

Generous employee pensions are ancient history, and Social Security is becoming increasingly uncertain. The lifestyle of retirees is no longer leisure, golfing, fishing, and travel. In fact, the lifestyle for many retirees may be continued work.

The latest Census Statistics show that only one out of every ten Americans today is financially prepared to retire when he or she reaches the age of sixty-five.

What about the current economic situation? As we know, the economy is in a recession; companies continue to cut staff in great numbers. You may as well kiss true job security good-bye. It does not seem to exist anymore.

Even if you are one of the lucky few who make it to retirement and manage to hang on to their jobs, the Bureau of Labor Statistics estimates that only 5 percent will have enough money to retire at age sixty-five.

This means that the standard route of working a traditional job has failed for 95 percent of all Americans. Shouldn't you, then, seriously re-evaluate the traditional career/job/employment scenario in order to get through retirement financially sound?

Here's the real kicker: You and most of the people you know are going to work for at least thirty to forty years—at jobs you hate—with bosses you hate—with commutes you hate—with hours that you hate. What a life—failing while you are miserable most of the time. Do you want to do this for the next forty years?

1.7 Are We Going in the Wrong Direction without a Map?

The fact that only 2 percent of the population is financially successful shows the need for a simple explanation. We need a global, twenty-first-century, scientific explanation of the law of attraction instead of a handful of controversial interpretations that continue to narrow down the opportunity to fewer individuals.

I am sure you will agree that such a low percentage of success indicates that the great majority, or 98 percent of the population, is undeniably *going in the wrong direction without a map*. It appears that attaining financial wealth involves highly complex formulas that only the few with the smarts and the opportunity can access. This distortion of facts shows up frequently, directly and indirectly, in all published materials. You can find books on just about any aspect of attaining financial wealth. You can pick up a copy of any of these books, and somewhere in your reading, you will find obstacles. The information is too complicated, or unclear, or just plain unbelievable. The end result is discouragement. In some cases, you decide to experiment and try whatever the book tells you to do for a few weeks, but in the back of your mind, you think it is not going to work—and you fail.

The collective debt of the average individual American is $233,263, slightly more than one quarter of a million dollars. This is a financially catastrophe with no end in sight.

Here is the breakdown of that one quarter of a million plus dollars:[4]

National Debt per citizen:	$38,366
United States spending per citizen:	9,647
Private debt per citizen:	24,448
Unfunded liability per citizen:	192,263
Total debt per citizen:	$233,077
Unemployed:	19,223,233
Bankruptcies:	1,068,889
United States National Debt:	$11,801,366,526,077

We are currently experiencing what is probably the worst financial crisis in the history of the United States; just looking at these numbers makes you feel hopeless.

1.8 Is it Deception or Denial?

Foreclosures, bankruptcies, large business going out of business, unemployment, automobile plants closing down, government trying to rescue the economy.

Many people think the current financial crisis is a direct result of the political climate in this country. But once you buy into this concept, you just bought a seat in the 98 percent group. If you want financial success, you cannot look to the government to save you; historically, successful entrepreneurs have not looked for the help of the government in making their fortunes. Financial success is your responsibility. Don't let national issues distract you from what's happening in your own mind and in your own life.

We are too busy with our lives, trying to live from paycheck to paycheck, and the most efficient way to keep abreast of what is going on is to rely on the media to answer our issues or concerns. It is human nature to find solutions to our problems by using whatever self-serving means are available to us. Understanding how the media works is not nuclear science. This is a media-driven society, and the media are driven by economics. Newspapers, radio, and television all use the same marketing techniques and strategies to get your attention. The primary function of the media is to create awareness of whatever awful, negative situations are happening at the moment; that is what sells newspapers and increases television ratings. Television programs are engaged in an ongoing struggle to get the highest ratings possible. The higher the ratings, the more money the networks can charge sponsors for commercials spots. The ultimate result, and the concern, is that the average American buys whatever is told to him or her, without any hesitation or question. It is a multi-billion dollar business with only one objective: to get your attention. In 1999, the stock trading company, E*TRADE, purchased a thirty-second Super Bowl commercial spot in which two guys and a chimpanzee clapped their hands to the Mexican song "La Cucaracha" out of the back of a trailer truck. The commercial ended with a sign saying, "We just wasted two million dollars." You can find this humorous commercial on YouTube.[5] Imagine a company spending two million dollars to get your attention for thirty seconds.

This is either a highly intelligent commercial or the biggest waste of money you have ever seen. The truth is, aside from the humorous content, it was a highly intelligent commercial. This company became one of the largest stock trading companies in the country by targeting 98 percent of the population. Imagine a chimp trying to get the average individual to invest money in a process where even highly trained experts lose their shirts.

The great majority of the time, everything directed to the 98 percent consumer group has a psychologically deceptive "stealth" tone, very much like the great magician that has you focusing all of your attention on his right hand while his left hand removes your wallet from your pocket. The company in this case amuses you with a completely pointless commercial that has nothing to do with investing. A manipulative deception? If you cannot see that, you are in denial.

If you want to become successful as an individual, you must ignore group ideologies such as "It's the government's fault" or "The answers to all of our problems can be found in a Super Bowl commercial." Ignore the media and look within yourself. The best way to get out of the 98 percent group is to trigger your own potential. Success is an internal process.

1.10 Rites of Passage

You actually start out your life belonging to whichever group your parents belong to. Then you get older and become part of the workforce. Even if you were born into the upper 2 percent group, you will most likely be drafted into the 98 percent group if, through some unpleasant circumstance, you do not wind up with a trust fund or a cushy job at Mommy and Daddy's company. At some point, almost everyone becomes responsible for his or her own financial success.

By the same token, if you were born in the 98 percent group, you could very well wind up in the 2 percent group, enjoying life while someone who grew up in the 2 percent group cleans your windshield for a dollar. It's all up to you.

1.11 Do You Think People are Successful by Accident?

If you are a hardworking individual who dreams of being successful one day, you may wonder why only a few individuals constantly achieve their dreams and seem to always do the right thing and be in the right place at the right time. You deserve to know that nothing of the kind happens by accident. You find your path completely on your own and most surprisingly, it is a neurological biochemical process, which uses the same brain structures, neurological chemicals, and pathways in the creation of any behavioral or substance addiction. Take a moment to think about this: Did I just say that the brain structures that can cause a substance abuse such as heroin addiction are the same structures that can cause the behavioral addiction to success? You need to take as much time as you need to clearly understand and incorporate the information I just gave you; it is a crucial part to understanding the problem and the 98 percent solution.

CHAPTER 2
The Laws of the Universe

2.1 The Law of Attraction Defined

The law of attraction, simply put, states that you can affect your future simply by thinking about it. If you think positively, you are more likely to experience positive outcomes. If you think negatively, you are more likely to experience negative outcomes. It's that simple, but understanding how it works and learning to take advantage of it can be considerably more complex.

As you learned in Chapter 1, 98 percent of the population has yet to attain financial success. This is in part because the law of attraction is frequently misunderstood. Many people continue to think the law of attraction is a form of spiritual harmonious alignment with the universe. Some say it dates back to six to seven thousand years ago, and some say it is manifested through the creative energy of the universe. Still others say the concept is modern, taken from updated versions of ideas discovered in ancient teachings and kept secret, only available to a chosen few very successful individuals. Some think it has a religious connection with a supreme force. These misleading and contradictory interpretations have created controversy and polarization. Aside from who is right or wrong, we all need to work with one simple understanding.

No one knows for certain why the law of attraction works. But regardless of where the law came from and regardless of its exact nature, I do know that it is important—and just as powerful as people claim it to be.

The law of attraction is very much a part of our daily lives. This law applies and operates every time on every person and every culture—including you. No matter who you are or where you are from, you begin to harness the power of the law of attraction the instant you create a thought. Thoughts can be positive or negative in nature; it is extremely important to note that our mindsets can have an enormous influence on any type of outcome. This is why an individual involved in the process of thinking about, creating, and pursuing specific positive goals appears to be very successful in all phases of life.

While this book focuses on financial success, the law of attraction does not apply to money. No matter how you quantify and measure success—in the number of projects you complete, in how many prestigious national awards you win, in how many hours of free time you enjoy a week, in how many times you make a loved one smile, or simply in how many meals you manage to put on the table—the law of attraction will help you. This law applies to any goal a person can have, financial or otherwise.

In other words, this is a universal law that works in the same way as the laws of mathematics. It is incredibly powerful, and anyone on the planet has the potential to benefit from it. So why haven't you? Why hasn't 98 percent of the population?

Unfortunately, the law of attraction is still a foreign concept to many people. You and many others might still be unsure how to use this law to your advantage. The law of attraction cannot necessarily be considered common sense; expecting the general public to intuitively grasp these ideas is like expecting a caveman to understand how a plane can fly across the sky. "You see, jet propulsion creates a controlled nuclear explosion that allows us to fly across the sky at up to 17,880 miles an hour!" you might explain cheerfully. Meanwhile, your new friend, the caveman, hasn't absorbed a word you've said, because to him, you are talking nonsense, and he is busy wondering whether the time machine that spit you out a moment ago is going to try to eat him next.

The simple truth is that sometimes, seeing is believing. Unfortunately, we cannot see intangible forces. For example, when an image comes in through the eyes and is projected onto the **visual cortex**, the image is converted into a complex set of neurological chemicals to form a chemical image pattern to be stored as a set of neuronal connections. All of this happens at the speed of 400 million bits per second. This concept is hard to swallow and digest. If it is not tangible and you cannot see it with your own eyes, the explanation will be slow in coming.

The good news is that forces invisible to the naked eye can still be observed indirectly. We may not be able to see gravity, but we can see the effects of gravity; we can personally witness how a pencil we've dropped is pulled toward the ground and held there.

Similarly, you may not be able to see the law of attraction in motion before your eyes, but in time, you will be able to see the financial benefits it brings you. In fact, if you follow my instructions, you will be convinced of the power of the law of attraction much sooner than you might think.

Even with today's modern science, we are still struggling with universal laws and concepts. The law of attraction continues to be a primary example of backwoods concepts and the center of controversy.

Even after this book is published and it creates a scientific paradigm, the law of attraction will be observed, probed, and scrutinize; I welcome the challenge. There will be individuals who will greatly benefit and individuals who take opposite points of view in their interpretations.

Of course, refusing to believe in the power of the law of attraction doesn't exempt someone from its effects. Evidence is mounting that the law of attraction exists, so instead of wasting your energy on skepticism while your misuse of the law of attraction prevents you from reaching your goals, it makes much more sense to open your mind and explore the possibilities that could arise from making the law of attraction work for you. After all, you have nothing to lose.

How is it possible to create reality simply by thinking about it? This chapter will examine the science behind the law of attraction. After all, unless you believe the law of attraction will work, you will have difficulty attaining the optimism required to generate positive outcomes for yourself. The good news is, plenty of scientific evidence exists to support the law of attraction. If you keep an open mind as you peruse this chapter, you might be surprised at how logical this supposedly mystical and magical law will begin to seem.

2.2 Other Useful Fundamental Laws of the Universe

While my method of achieving financial success does not require you to comprehend any fancy equations or complicated formulas, it might be helpful to take a look at a few basic and relevant laws of physics, explained as simply as possible.

These are the laws that govern the world around us with precision. Let us briefly talk about some of these laws and how they pertain to us.

The laws of motion:

First law: A body persists its state of rest or of uniform motion unless acted upon by an external unbalanced force. Newton's first law is often referred to as the *law of inertia*.

When you hit a baseball with a bat, friction from the air slows the ball down, and gravity pulls it toward the earth. If it weren't for such intervening forces, the game of baseball would be much more boring for the outfield players, since the baseball would simply sail into the sky and keep on going.

Second law: Force equals mass times acceleration ($\mathbf{F} = m\mathbf{a}$). The net force on an object is equal to the mass of the object multiplied by its acceleration.

In plain old English, this law is making the observation if you are rearranging your bookshelves, a smaller bookshelf would require less energy to move across the room than a larger one. Also, if you are in a hurry to rearrange everything, the amount of force you have to put behind any bookshelf as you lean on it and push it across the room is going to have to increase if you want your speed to increase.

Third law: To every action there is an equal and opposite reaction.

When you step forward off a skateboard, your other foot will push the skateboard backward a little. The rolling of the skateboard backward is the opposite reaction to your action of taking a step forward.

Laws of thermodynamics:

First law of thermodynamics: Energy can neither be created nor destroyed. It can only change forms in any process in an isolated system; the total energy remains the same. This First Law states that energy cannot be created or destroyed; the amount of energy lost in a steady-state process cannot be greater than the amount of energy gained. This is the statement of conservation of energy for a thermodynamic system. It refers to the two ways that a closed system transfers energy to and from its surroundings—by the process of heating (or cooling) and by the process of mechanical work. The rate of gain or loss in the stored energy of a system is determined by the rates of these two processes. In open systems, the flow of matter is another energy-transfer mechanism, and extra terms must be included in the expression of the first law.

Second law of thermodynamics: Put simply, the second law states that "energy systems have a tendency to increase their entropy rather than decrease it." The word "entropy" refers to a trend toward disorganization; heat is more likely to spread out than bunch together. This can also be stated as "heat can spontaneously flow from a higher-temperature region to a lower-temperature region, but not the other way around." (Heat *can* flow from cold to hot, but not spontaneously—for example, when a refrigerator expends electrical power.)

A way for non-scientists to think about the second law is to consider entropy as a measure of ignorance of the microscopic details of the system. So, for example, one has less knowledge about the separate fragments of a broken cup than about an intact one, because when the fragments are separated, one does not know exactly whether they will fit together again, or whether perhaps there is a missing shard.

Third law of Thermodynamics: As temperature approaches absolute zero, the entropy of a system approaches a constant minimum. Briefly, this postulates that entropy is temperature dependent and results in the formulation of the idea of absolute zero.

Tentative fourth laws or principles: Most fourth-law statements are speculative and controversial. The most commonly proposed Fourth Law concerns the Onsager relations, which give a quantitative relationship between the parameters of a system in which heat and matter are simultaneously flowing. Most variations of hypothetical fourth laws (or principles) have to do with the environmental sciences, biological evolution, or **galactic phenomena**.[6]

Laws of chemistry:

Avogadro's Law: Equal volumes of gases under identical temperature and pressure conditions will contain equal numbers of particles (atoms, ions, molecules, electrons, etc.)

Boyle's Law: At constant temperature, the volume of a confined gas is inversely proportional to the pressure to which it is subjected. PV = k.

Charles's Law: At constant pressure, the volume of a confined gas is directly proportional to the absolute temperature. V = kT.

Dalton's Law: The pressure of a mixture of gases is equal to the sum of the partial pressures of the component gases.

Definite Composition: A compound is composed of two or more elements chemically combined in a defined ratio by weight.

Dulong & Petit's Law: Most metals require 6.2 cal of heat in order to raise the temperature of 1 gram of atomic mass of the metal by 1°C.

Faraday's Law: The weight of any element liberated during electrolysis is proportional to the quantity of electricity passing through the cell and also to the equivalent weight of the element.

Gay-Lussac's Law: The ratio between the combining volumes of gases and the product (if gaseous) can be expressed in small whole numbers.

Graham's Law: The rate of effusion or diffusion of a gas is inversely proportional to the square root of its molecular mass.

Henry's Law: The solubility of a gas (unless it is highly soluble) is directly proportional to the pressure applied to the gas.

Ideal Gas Law: The state of an ideal gas is determined by its pressure, volume, and temperature according to the equation: $pV = nRT$

Periodic Law: The chemical properties of the elements vary periodically according to their atomic numbers.

The law of gravity: Under an assumption of constant gravity, Newton simplifies to $F = mg$, where m is the mass of the body and g is a constant vector with an average magnitude of 9.81 m/s^2. The acceleration due to gravity is equal to this g. An initially-stationary object which is allowed to fall freely under gravity drops a distance which is proportional to the square of the elapsed time.

And our main focus, the law of attraction: From the pseudo scientific description of *positive attracts positive and negative attracts negative* redefined to the scientific description, *negative creates negative and positive creates positive.* This definition is in compliance with true scientific research in anatomical neurological biochemical functions of the human. Once you create thoughts of a positive nature the mind will continue to manifest the thoughts as long as the thoughts continue to be positive and there is no interference with the production of certain chemicals in the body to continue the direction of creating. (This process is explained in greater detail in section 3.1 and in Chapter 4, "The Biology of Belief.") This can also happen with negative thoughts. The introduction of a negative thought can halt the production of desirable chemicals and cause an unwanted result.

Determining which laws are more important than others is not a simple task. To gain at least a general notion, we can focus on the one the law that keeps us from floating away into space, the law of gravity, which is the natural phenomenon by which objects with mass attract one another. In everyday life, gravitation is most commonly thought of as the law that lends weight to objects with mass. Gravitation compels dispersed matter to come together and unite, thus accounting for the existence of the earth, the sun, and most of the macroscopic objects in the universe. It is responsible for keeping the earth and the other planets in their orbits around the sun; for keeping the moon in its orbit around the earth; and for the formation of tides. Modern physics describes gravitation using the general **theory of relativity**, in which gravitation is a consequence of the curvature of space-time, which governs the motion of inertial objects.

However vague or specific that may sound to you, I will extend a simplified version of the explanation. This law is the reason objects accelerate toward Earth at a speed of 9.8 meters per second squared. This important universal law dictates that if you jump off the tenth floor of a building, it is quite certain your direction of travel will be down and not up, and unless you quickly learn how to fly, you will hit the ground and become a human waffle.

We do not have time to mention any of the other laws because it is beyond the scope of this material, but we will intently focus and direct our full attention to the law of attraction, the law that engages every individual in his or her unconscious and conscious thought process. It is an integral part of our thinking process, and it guides our motivational and creative processes. This law integrates our thoughts with the creative parts of our minds to manifest the thoughts into reality. Remember, everything and anything you think about is attracted to you by default. Once you focus your attention and understand this precept, it requires constant ongoing practice. When you are ready to move on to Chapter 5, you will learn about operant conditioning, and Chapter 6 will teach you how to put operant conditioning into practice, and without hesitation or doubt, create radical changes in your life.

2.3 What Is Real?

Quantum physics is the study of possibilities—this is what Thomas J. McFarlane has to say about this very interesting subject as he tries to interpret other experts' opinions. Read the following excerpts from McFarlane's article "Quantum Mechanics and Reality"[7]

> Werner Heisenberg, the inventor of **quantum mechanics** has this to say about reality:
>
> > If one wants to give an accurate description of the elementary particle the only thing, which can be written down as, description is a probability function. But then one sees that not even the quality of being belongs to what is described.
>
> Now read what Niels Bohr, the pioneer of twentieth-century physics has to say about reality:
>
> > An independent reality, in the ordinary physical sense, can neither be ascribed to the phenomena nor to the agencies of observation.
>
> These people make the outrageous claim that we normally live in the **delusion** that there is a real, objective world. Since this seems to be in blatant contradiction with both our immediate experience and everything most of us were ever taught, our natural response is to dismiss it as ludicrous.

Essentially, McFarlane, Heisenberg, and Bohr are saying that we do not have the ability to establish that the "real world" even exists; there is no proven reality beyond our own perceptions. In fact, a key discovery in quantum mechanics is that our thoughts and observations can actually shape and affect the reality that we once thought existed completely independently of us. In other words, reality is in the eye of the beholder; the mere act of thinking about something can actually bring it into existence. Scientific evidence exists that our thoughts affect reality. For instance, Rollin McCraty, PhD, the Director of Research at the Institute of HeartMath, has conducted experiments showing that simply by remembering an embarrassing moment, we can affect the electrical activity in nearby bacteria. Our thoughts have power.

McFarlane goes on to give an analogy that may help us to understand the limits of our understanding:

> For a typical modern Westerner, it might be easy to dismiss the radical claims of a few isolated mystics. But can we dismiss the physicists so easily? Niels Bohr and Werner Heisenberg are legends of 20th century science. Nobel Prize winners. They are the creators of quantum mechanics, the most precise and far-reaching physical theory ever devised. It explains how the sun shines, how molecules bond together, how iron is magnetized, and even why objects are hard. This is the physics that gives us computer chips, lasers, and atomic bombs. So to dismiss quantum mechanics is to throw out the cornerstone of modern physics and the basic theory at the foundation of all these modern wonders. If we are to be honest with ourselves, we had better think twice before dismissing what Bohr and Heisenberg have to say and take a closer look.

> Our experience, for the most part, conforms to the idea that there really is an objective world out there. Most of us take thousands of objects to be real every day and find that there is no contradiction with experience at all. Nevertheless, both the mystics and the physicists claim that the objective world is an illusion. But if this common sense idea of an objective world is wrong, why does it seem so right? To shed some light on this question and its answer, let us digress for a moment and consider the following scenario.

> Imagine going back in time 3000 years and encountering people convinced that the world is really a flat disc. When you hear this you tell them that they are mistaken, that the world is really round.

But you become quite embarrassed when they ask you to prove it to them and you find that you cannot. After all, their experience conforms to the idea that the earth is really flat. They measure out land and make road maps using plane geometry and never find any contradiction with experience at all. So your claim that the earth is really round sounds to them like a delusion and they dismiss you as a crazy mystic—especially when you start telling them about people from your time who ascend into the heavens in a blaze of fire where they are able to look down upon the whole created world and actually see that it is round. So you get back in your time machine and head back home to the future.[8]

We have to continue our search for knowledge and closely pursue science with an open mind. Science will provide us with functional answers to all of our questions.

Any number of differences between two people can determine their respective individual realities. The colorblind person can only process certain colors. If you showed two individuals, one colorblind and one not, a red car, each would have a different reality of the car. Each individual's perception of the car would be different; reality becomes the person's perception of his or her surroundings.

If all reality is an illusion, then we have no answers to some very common questions. Who are you? Where do you come from? Where are you going? How are you going? Why are you here? How did you get here? A functional answer to these questions can be reached for the first time through the neurological biochemical model, which accommodates the principle that reality is an individual's perception; in other words, reality is in the eye of the beholder. All neurological biochemical research shows that from the moment information leaves the visual cortex of the occipital lobes for further processing in the **associative regions,** the interpretation of reality is unique to each individual's making. What is real to you may not be real to me.

The law of attraction can be understood in religious terms if a person is religious. The point is that the law of attraction can be explained differently by either a religious person or a scientist, but the neurological biochemical response will be the same: feeling good produces positive thoughts, which makes us feel good; feeling bad produces negative thoughts, which make us feel bad. It does not matter what the person's educational or religious background is as long as the brain structures are the same. A scientist might be more inclined to understand the quantum mechanics explanation, while a religious person will be more inclined to understand the religious explanation. The explanations are completely different, but each is in line with the person's reality. It is beyond the scope of this book to prove or disprove any theories. We can only limit our opinions according to our level of understanding. Further research into available scientific evidence could lead to a clearer understanding of whether what we see is real or an illusion. To say the analysis of the fathers of quantum mechanics is incorrect is to say all of the inventions of the modern world were accidents and made by mad scientists.

The model to help you understand is clear, simple, and late in coming. Buy a simple DVD player and it comes with 150-page instruction book. When I picked up each of my newborns, I remember getting a baby wrapped in a blanked with a hospital pacifier and that was it; the operational manual was missing. Science has been writing this operational manual for some time; we are now able to understand some of the complex reactions that go on inside the brain. Once you do understand some of these operations, you will realize reality is our own illusion, from start to finish. Every visual cue coming into our brain is transformed into a series of chemical reactions and assembled into our own interpretation—or our illusion. That is as good an explanation as we can get. The earth is round and not flat. We do jump into a vehicle that uses a controlled nuclear explosion for traveling across the heavens; who are we to argue? The pictures show the earth is undoubtedly round.

If the reality is created by the self, then it is safe to say that you create the same reality for yourself day after day by creating the same relationships, the same types of friends, the same scenarios, the same difficulties, the same problems, the same behavior, the same maladaptive behaviors, and the same types of jobs, over and over. What you may not have realized is that you have millions of other choices with infinite possibilities for change. Day after day, you continue to create the same realities—often carbon copies of the previous realities. Is that what you really want? If not, it is time to become aware of the other possibilities. If we do not acknowledge that the reality was created through trial and error, we lose control, become more mired in our own defective realities, and settle for mediocrity.

For an example of how this works, let's take a look at Sally, a resident of Middletown, U.S.A. Sally is an imaginary person full of thoughts and habits that could be considered ordinary.

Every day, when Sally's alarm goes off in the morning, she rolls out of bed, staggers into the shower, and then spends an hour of her morning reading the paper and drinking coffee before she heads off to work. She tosses the thick newspaper into the recycling bin on her way out the door before she climbs into her Land Rover.

Sally is a networking technician for a small law firm in a small town. She has worked there for a decade, and she enjoys the job. When Sally returns home from work, she eats dinner and then relaxes while engaging in her nightly ritual of watching soap operas that her digital video recorder has stored up for her; she does this so they don't pile up and cause her to fall behind. The next day, she does it all over again.

It's hard to say how Sally developed this routine. There is certainly nothing objectionable about the routine, and perhaps it truly represents the life that might make her the happiest. Does your opinion of her routine change when you consider the following facts?

- Sally's husband, Bill, passed away two years ago after ten years of marriage.
- Both the morning coffee habit and the newspaper subscription originally belonged to her husband; Sally began enjoying the ritual with him as part of their married life.
- Sally's reading of the paper in the morning has less to do with her love of current events and more to do with an absentminded desire to avoid falling behind; without her husband, the papers had really started piling up in the kitchen. In reality, Sally is the sort of person who would more likely enjoy a chapter of a novel in the morning.
- The Land Rover is a car that she and her husband had picked out together; Bill had often enjoyed hunting trips and other outings, and the pair had planned to have children. Sally originally kept it for sentimental reasons. She no longer really thinks about it one way or the other, even though it gets bad gas mileage and is much larger than a single person might need.
- Sally could make a much better wage doing the same job at a larger firm in a different city.
- Sally originally moved to Middletown when her husband was transferred there. She has no family in Middletown, but continues to live there because she has been there for eight years and knows her way around.
- Sally gets a certain amount of satisfaction from deleting shows off her video recorder once she has watched them; it makes her feel neat, up-to-date, and organized.

Not every aspect of Sally's routine necessarily needs changing. Perhaps she now loves coffee as much as her husband used to, and perhaps she enjoys her soap operas enough to continue watching them at night instead of engaging in other activities. But one running theme is obvious: a great deal of Sally's routine was formed as part of her marriage to Bill. Some of it, such as the reading of the newspaper, may be continuing as a result of Sally's sense that she is on a treadmill and must keep up with that routine—in other words, Sally may have fallen victim to inertia in her life.

If Sally really grasped the idea that she might make twenty thousand dollars more a year in another city, she might be willing to learn her way around a new place, but a great deal of Sally's life is based on habit. She enjoyed a decade of marriage, and during that time, she made compromises that have caused her to forget some of her own dreams and personal preferences. Unless she makes an active effort to examine her life to see whether it lines up with her goals, she may continue to create the same day for herself over and over, even if that day has become obsolete without her husband around to share it with her.

Some of this routine may have been established based on Sally's grief and continuing feelings for her husband. What happened within Sally led to the creation of her routine. What happens within us creates our reality.

To add to this confusing perception of reality, a question arises again: do we see with our brain or do we see with our eyes? The truth is that the brain does not know the difference between what it sees and what it can remember because both situations operate under the same neurological network. The answer then, is that what we see as reality is our own perception and a composition of our emotions and thoughts, all created by the billions of connections that create our neural net to form our personality.

In this complex system, we can identify thought processes that limit our potential. This may be the answer to why a small percentage of the population is successful. I will mention the limitations and you can decide what the possibilities are.

Our sense organs are in a constant state of awareness and a huge amount of information is coming from all directions. The brain processes three hundred to four hundred million bits of information per second, but we are only aware of two to three thousand bits because information is filtered to our consciousness to monitor only time, our surroundings, and our body. That means information is coming into the brain but the filters do not allow the integration of all of the millions of bits the brain is receiving.

2.4 Does Your Head Hurt Yet?

If you are struggling with how some of the universal laws presented in this chapter work, don't stress. Just because humanity doesn't have an explanation for something right at this moment, that doesn't mean no explanation exists.

For instance, consider the aurora borealis (also known as the northern lights). We now know that this dazzling display is the result of the emission of photons in the earth's upper atmosphere. But in the Middle Ages, the northern lights were considered a sign from God, and various Native American tribes considered them to be spiritual events.

This book offers an explanation of how the law of attraction works; the idea is that understanding the biological and scientific mechanisms behind the law of attraction might increase your trust in the power of thinking positively.

But if you struggle to grasp these explanations, do not get frustrated. What appears to be magical or **supernatural** often has a logical explanation, but that doesn't mean you are required to understand it just to benefit from it. Regardless of the explanation, what really matters is that your approach helps you accomplish your dreams.

2.5 The Law of Attraction: A Universal Phenomenon

Everyone without exception is under the influence of the law of attraction. It is an everyday occurrence and part of our everyday thinking process, both conscious and unconscious. This is the law that most influences our thoughts, ideas, motivation, and creativity.

The key to changing your behavior patterns and thinking is your understanding of this law of attraction, which can be a very difficult concept to understand at first. My goal and major responsibility is to be able to clearly explain to you the process so that you too can put it into practice just as many individuals have done in the past.

In my explanation, I am going to include many disciplines, such as psychology, **neuropsychology**, **molecular biology**, neurological biology, biochemistry, behavioral sciences, quantum mechanics, and physics. Do not let any of these subjects scare you; I will assume all of the responsibility for your understanding of content, knowledge, and concepts. It will all come together for you at the end of your reading.

Through no fault of your own, some of you will have to read this book multiple times and apply greater effort to understand because the average person has been conditioned to accept life the way it is. Conditioning is discussed in more depth in Chapter 5, but essentially, it refers to the formation of a habit. Even giving up can be a habit, as is the case in those conditioned to failure.

This conditioning to accept life the way it is becomes our main area of difficulty in making major life-changing corrections. Take a personal inventory or inventory of someone close to you and see how we all have a tendency to follow the same patterns in life over and over again. We tend to find the same types of relationships, seek the same types of jobs, and exhibit the same maladaptive behavior, without any awareness or internal system of correction.

It is safe to say the majority of individuals tend to go through life on autopilot. The bad news is the older you are, the more conditioned you are to your environment and surroundings. The good news is that conditioning is reversible.

The law of attraction is completely under your control. You can condition your thoughts for failure or success, with failure taking less of an effort.

What conditioned circumstances, or bad habits, could you change in your own life? Do you work at a dead-end job? Do you live from paycheck to paycheck? What aspects of your life could be more efficient, more enjoyable, or more profitable? No one's life is perfect, and anyone stands to benefit from the law of attraction—including you.

Plato, Shakespeare, Newton, Dalton, Beethoven, Einstein, Lincoln, and Edison are just a few of the famous individuals we can study and analyze how they applied the law of attraction in their contributions to the world.

History shows they all have one thing in common, and they all believed and understood the law of attraction. Some made attempts to explain to others how the law of attraction worked for them but failed to provide clear explanations for the average individual to understand. We often think their contributions put them in a category above everyone else, but in reality, they were no different from any one of us. Every one of them experienced the same problems we all experience and the same difficulties going through their particular time in life.

Who would have thought that the most celebrated scientist of all time dropped out of high school and was not accepted into the university because he failed the entrance exam, forcing him back to high school?

If we analyze a few current successful individuals, we will find they are no smarter than you or I.

The highly successful author J.K. Rowling wrote a series of very popular books about kids with supernatural powers. The books were made into movies, and as a result, she is one of the wealthiest women in the world.

Stephanie Meyer, another amazingly successful writer, wrote another series of popular books about vampires. Two of the books have been made into movies, and Meyer enjoys great financial wealth as a result of her creativity. I have nothing but total admiration for her creative thought process. She took a subject theme line that has been recycled in Hollywood films for decades and brought it onto center stage again.

Steve Jobs, the cofounder and CEO of Apple, Inc., started his business in his garage and is now responsible for running one of the most successful computer companies in the world. Michael Dell, the founder of Dell, Inc., started building computers in his college dormitory and wound up as the chief executive officer of another famous brand of computers.

The most impressive of all is Bill Gates, the individual that dropped out of Harvard in his sophomore year and became involved in the introduction of one of the most important advances in computer software technology. He is responsible for the operating system that the majority of Americans use in their computers.

You may ask yourself what all of these people have in common. They all have one thing in common—the law of attraction. You become what you think you can be, or thoughts become actions. Success was not handed to any one of them; they made it happen.

We have been trying to understand how thoughts turn into an actions since 1879, when the *New York Times* became the first major newspaper to use the phrase "law of attraction," describing the wagon trains of the Colorado gold rush as "moving in obedience to some occult law of attraction that overcomes all obstacles in their progress to their destination."

In 1902, John Ambrose Fleming, an electrical engineer, described it as the formation of matter through an indescribable physical internal energy guiding our personal growth. He referred to it as an unquenchable *energy of attraction* steadily increasing the process of growth until completion of the desired outcome.

In 1907, the law of attraction was a byproduct of a *new thought movement* that gained popularity, saying the action of the mind is centered around a nucleus, which if allowed to grow undisturbed, will attract the thought to be manifested as a reality.

Another individual, William Walker Atkinson, tried explaining it as a *thought vibration*. It then became known as prosperity through *thought force*, summarized as "You are what you think, not what you think you are."

In 1915, the law of attraction became part of the **Theosophical** movement.

In 1937, *Think and Grow Rich* was published; it was then that the law of attraction began to focus on the importance of controlling your *thoughts* to achieve success. The direction became more of an interpretation, referring to positive energy and the secret to success. This was the first time this process was described as a *secret* kept from the population.

From the 1900s to 2000, the law was referred to by multiple disciplines, using religious, occult, and secular terms, such as positive thinking, metaphysics, new thought, the science of the mind, religious science and divine intervention.

The twentieth-century authors referred to it as a certain state of mind that could produce *medical healing*. Today, people speak of the power of positive thought in medicine, and everyone accepts the placebo effect in pharmaceutical research.

In the twenty-first century, the law of attraction gained widespread popularity with a movie called *The Secret.* The success of the film and various books led to increased media coverage. The movie was featured on *The Oprah Winfrey Show*, on two separate occasions, and on *The Larry King Show.* As a result of media coverage, the law of attraction gained negative attention. Talk show host Larry King criticized it for several reasons. He pointed to the sufferings in the world and asked, "If the universe manifests abundance at a mere thought, why is there so much poverty, starvation, and death?" The truth is, of course, that not everyone is using the law of attraction to his or her benefit, and the law of attraction influences events rather than completely controlling them, so the existence of the law of attraction does not preclude negative events.

Now, as a neuropsychologist, I am redefining the law of attraction from "negative attracts negative and positive attracts positive" to "negative creates negative and positive creates positive." This description clarifies all of the *backwoods concepts* and explains the law as not a product of the occult or supernatural, not magnetic energy or vibration; it is not divine intervention, metaphysical, or a religious science. It is learned behavioral operant conditioning explained through our own neurological biochemical process to be able to create a thought, shape it through **consequences,** and reinforce it with the desired outcome. Once the desired outcome is attained, **reinforcement** occurs—in other words, the behavior that resulted in the outcome becomes more likely to be repeated in the future. Repetition results in behavioral conditioning. The level of difficulty decreases with each reinforcing trial.

Let us clear up the Larry King criticism. Success is a relative term. I do not know much about Larry King. However, from my point of view he has been operating with the law of attraction for many years. If I were ever invited to appear on *The Larry King Show*, the first thing I would do would be to ask Mr. King to define what success is to him. If he answered having good health, a very attractive spouse, money in the bank, nice homes, nice cars, good friends, strong solid investments, popularity, and success on television, then I would venture to say that his achievements are the result of very hard work for many years, persevering relentlessly and diligently in the pursuit of success. This is the result of operant conditioning through a process of consequences, all reinforced by achieving his goals. Mr. King is a prime example of an individual using the law of attraction. The same is true for Oprah Winfrey. If an invitation ever came for me to be on her show, my first question to Oprah would be: How could one little person achieve so much in one lifetime? Oprah is the poster child for and an excellent example of how the law of attraction works. A careful analysis of this powerful media icon shows her drive (consequence) to help others (stimulus) has provided huge levels of success (reinforcement). A process that has happened over and over again shows she has been conditioned to be successful. That is why everything she touches turns to gold.

Millions of people desperately want to learn how all of this works, but unfortunately this backwoods concept has made it very difficult for people to grasp this intangible concept.

The law of attraction states thoughts become things. Learn how this works and it operates in harmony with abundance; however, success is a relative term. Success for Larry King may not the same as success for an individual in Tanzania, where it could mean having enough food on the table for one day to feed his family.

The major emphasis is to take notice and use the methods to achieve our full potential. What makes all of this possible is we do not all want the same things in life. Every individual has his or her own unique, diversified catalog of events, and all we need is to pick from our own catalog and place our order. How much time it takes for it to manifest depends on our relentless effort and time we devote to its manifestation.

2.6 The Creation of Success

Imagine yourself in a roomful of science students having one of the most celebrated scientists of all time explain the theory of relativity. The average individual will be lost by the time he explains the first equation.

We do not have to understand equations or formulas; undoubtedly, most individuals cannot, will not, and do not relate well to physics. The great majority would find Einstein's lecture boring, but the part we can certainly find interesting and understand is how it all came together for him.

During his teen years, Einstein began with an interest in the properties and behavior of light. At sixteen, he came up with a theory that light is always traveling at the same speed and is constant, rather than wavelike, as was thought at the time. He also proposed that it was not possible to travel faster than the speed of light (186,000 miles per second).

Time, on the other hand, is not constant, according to Einstein. In fact, it passed more slowly the faster one went. The faster you travel, the more time slows down for you—even if you don't feel any different. Believe it or not, when you fly across the country on an airplane, you disembark just the tiniest bit younger than you would have been if you had simply stayed home.

How did Einstein come up with such remarkable theories that wound up making such a great contribution to society? He first started with a set of highly complicated thoughts to form a group of ideas, and after a great deal of motivation and an ongoing, long-term creativity, he achieved a very important milestone in the scientific community. My contribution is to help you understand the nature of this simple creative process. Even if you are no Einstein, you have the ability to emulate this process in order to make your own important achievements.

My oldest son was assigned a science project in middle school and parents were allowed to assist in the project. We decided we were going to explain Einstein's theory of time travel by demonstrating that traveling faster than the speed of light causes time to slow down. The explanation consisted of how time slows down in a model rocket when traveling faster than the speed of light from Earth to another planet. The theory states that time slows down as you approach the speed of light. Take a set of twins: One twin travels five years to a planet and five back, while the other twin stays on Earth. Ten years would have elapse in the spaceship while the twin that stayed on Earth would be twenty years older. The science teacher gave him a grade of excellent, but the project was not picked for the school science fair. I though the project had much merit and disagreed with the decision enough to send the teacher a note asking for an explanation. The teacher wrote me back a brief note saying, "We all know that time travel is not possible." That incident and similar ones throughout my career have made me a better educator.

My son's teacher had refused to maintain an open mind, even when scientifically established facts were involved—and this is a professional educator we're talking about! If you refuse to keep your mind open to new information that might contradict what you currently believe, you are doomed to remain stuck in whatever rut you currently occupy. Yet many people do refuse to consider new ideas or information, which explains why only 2 percent of the population experiences overwhelming success and the rest continues to live in mediocrity.

A large portion of 98 percent of the population could not achieve success even if it fell in their laps. A prime example of this is lottery winners. I was researching how to develop the million-dollar mindset and came across valuable information about lottery winners that reinforces the fact that if you do not have the mindset of the millionaire you will never achieve the goal. According to an article published in Lendingtree,[9] more than 80 percent of the individuals that win the lottery end up losing all their winnings by the fifth year, with some of the larger jackpot winners filing for bankruptcy.

If you ask yourself how can someone go through fifty or one hundred million dollars in that short a time, the answer is simple: It all boils down to the acquisition process. The winners' success did not come from within; they did not learn successful behaviors or positive thought patterns. They didn't have to work very hard for their huge payoff. Easy come, easy go.

Long-lasting, enduring, habitual success is not a product of luck. It actually starts as a thought and a complex set of ideas, which leads to the creation process. Everything is constructed by the individual as a result of a series of complex biochemical reactions, all formulated in the neurological net, all of the long- and short-term neural synaptic connections that form the personality. It is a step-by-step process, and the first step is to formulate the thought and have an intense and relentlessly constant focus on it. The creative part of you will find ways for its manifestation.

It is imperative to recognize that a positive thought (pride, desire, gratitude, hope, empathy, happiness, euphoria, or joy) will produce an emotionally good feeling. Since the brain does not discriminate between good and bad thoughts, the part that is under your control is the actual creation of the thought. Focusing on negative thoughts (jealousy, frustration, doubt, envy, despair, depression, sadness, shame, grief, fear or guilt) will create negative situations.

Observe individuals who are successful and notice how they always have a more positive outlook on life than those who are not. Those who complain the most always seem to live in a negative state of mind. Those who complain about their health are less healthy. Those who complain the most about their problems seem to have more.

If you think of good things that make you feel good always—good things will manifest 100 percent of the time without fail.

CHAPTER 3
You and the Law of Attraction

3.1 Attraction by Default

When you learn how to apply the law of attraction in your daily life, you will undoubtedly notice everything that happens to you, every situation good or bad, you are creating by default. For example, if you are in a situation where you are constantly working toward a goal, the goal will manifest. You may be attending college or trying to achieve an advanced degree. Perhaps you would like to get a new job or increase your stock portfolio. Maybe you're renting an apartment and you feel it's time to move up to a house, but you aren't sure how you will afford it. If you continue to work hard, it happens. If you fail to have the thoughts that promote the success, interference will take over and eventually you will drop out. So you can say you attract or create the circumstance by default At first it will be a very difficult concept to grasp, but without exception, everyone is able to benefit from its application. You may take longer than someone else does, but you will learn to produce the right biochemical results in your neurological net to create a correctional shift in your life.

Once you begin to be successful on a regular basis, you will notice a major critical factor to avoid in this formula is time. You must think you have all the time in the world in order to remove the pressure that time creates. You have to remove time from the equation. You cannot in any way limit or place any time constraints on your thoughts. If you do, you open up Pandora's box. If you place a time limit on a goal, you turn on the meter; the moment the time meter expires, the goal goes right into the brain's recycle bin and you have created a negative outcome by default.

Think about how many decades it took you to get to where you are now. Think about how unyielding, impenetrable, and solid your belief neurological connections are. Think about how many times you have tried something that did not materialize. Each goal you create has to have the identical, constant neurological biochemical production. You continue to persevere with the thought until it happens. A time constraint will put you immediately in the wrong frame of mind. I will later explain the neurological biochemical process of perseverance.

Thomas Edison's invention of the light bulb documents a history lesson in perseverance. Humphrey Davy invented the light bulb in 1809. However, everyone is under the impression that Thomas Edison was the original inventor. When Edison was asked why he failed so many times, he replied that he did not fail; he just found two thousand ways for the light bulb not to work.

3.2 The Underlying Process of a Thought

Let us direct our attention to feeling-good emotions (pride, desire, gratitude, hope, empathy, happiness, euphoria and joy) and feeling-bad emotions (jealousy, frustration, doubt, envy, despair, depression, sadness, shame, grief, fear and guilt). The same gland in your brain, the **hypothalamus,** produces both of these feelings. The hypothalamus is a peptide protein-producing factory. There are peptide chains of amino acids, each with a signature for the specific emotion being created. These are released into the bloodstream to target specific cells. It is important to know that the bad-feeling chemical peptide has a different structure than the good chemical peptide. We also know the targeted cells have all of the receptors needed to accommodate each chain. If a cell does not have enough, the next time that cell reproduces it includes more. The brain does not identify either feeling; it produces the chemicals to match the thought. It will respond the same way, with the same process, and in the same manner. We have to control the thought to have the appropriate production of peptide proteins.

How do you change from negative thoughts? The brain is bombarded with an enormous amount of information constantly coming in from all of our sense organs; an ongoing assessment is constantly taking place to determine what is important and what is not. The capacity to process at our level of awareness is restricted to only about two thousand bits (units of information) per second. The information is then transferred to the associative regions, or the part in the brain that interprets information at a much higher speed, which can process at the much higher rate of 300 to 400 million bits per second. The information as it comes in is restricted to two thousand bits per second for analysis. We can only see or be aware of what our personality belief system analyzes to be possible by constantly matching established patterns in the associative regions.

The key to a negative course correction is to regain control of the hypothalamus by creating the positive (again, these are pride, desire, gratitude, hope, empathy, happiness, euphoria, and joy) feeling-good-emotion chemical chain to produce the appropriate positive behavior and stop the behavioral response that creates or attracts more negative behavior.

It is important to understand how this procedure works, because unless you are in direct control of what needs to be done, you will be not be able to make any reversals or course corrections.

3.3 The Great Misconception

Volumes of books have been written on the subject of positive thinking. The overall message is to think positive thoughts and when a negative thought comes up, replace it with a positive one. This procedure was popular until we began to learn more about how the brain works chemically. Various scientific research has indicated that it is chemically impossible to replace a positive thought with a negative one. This is where the misconception starts. If you try to replace a negative thought (jealousy, frustration, doubt, envy, despair, depression, sadness, shame, grief, fear, or guilt) with a positive one (pride, desire, gratitude, hope, empathy, happiness, euphoria or joy), you will actually produce both types of peptide chains. This causes neutralization or interference, which stops the creative process. You can handle only one thought or the other.

Insightfully, we know that a person who is depressed has very little or no motivation at all to do anything. At a biochemical level, the production of feeling-bad emotional peptides are overwhelming and in the targeted cells, receptors are accommodating this intense production. Persistent conditions often lead to the need for medical biochemical psychopharmacology. A number of antidepressants are made to work directly on the cells to block receptors and stop depression. In most cases, this is the easiest route because the individual has sunk to huge and constant levels of this negative biochemical production, which not only stifle creativity and change but can produce other more severe physical symptoms.

3.4 Many Explanations, Many Disciplines

The scientific field of study surrounding the law of attraction is saturated with explanations and they all have the best intentions. Everyone wants you to understand it and is saying, in effect, "you have to try this; it is wonderful."

When the average person first tries to understand the law of attraction, he or she formulates many questions. Many individuals think it is all about magnetic fields: like attracts and negative repels. We then have the group with the positive and negative vibrations. The scholars weigh in with their discussion of whether everything is real or an illusion, and the **theologians** tell us we are all under one supreme force.

The truth is that all of these groups are imparting the truth. We are all under one supreme force. We are all carbon units made up of small particles with magnetic fields, and these particles do move and vibrate in space. We need to bring all of this down to a basic level of understanding so that the average person can understand it; otherwise, we continue to lose a good portion of the audience.

3.5 The Most Important Aspect of the Law of Attraction

No matter which explanation of the law of attraction you prefer, the fact remains that positive thoughts cause more positive thoughts—and, eventually, positive outcomes. Negative thoughts have the same power. If you expect to make your financial goals, it is very important to create positive thoughts. This is the most important thing to understand about the law of attraction, and you can use conditioning to reap its benefits.

The production of emotionally positive neurological biochemical produces more production of the same. On the other hand, production of emotionally negative neurological biochemical works in the same manner: more negative production occurs. The creative part of your personality only works with the positive production; negative production neutralizes and stops it.

3.6 How Does Negative Attract (Create) Negative and Positive Attract (Create) Positive?

One of the great mysteries in quantum mechanics is past, present, and future. We do not have the ability to predict the future, but we can make highly accurate guesses by carefully analyzing the past and the present. We know we do not have the ability to change the past, but we do have the ability to change the present. By changing the present, we can greatly affect the future. Go back ten years and think where you were then. Now look at the present—anything you change now will greatly affect your future. What if you had invested in a savings account instead of buying video games? You would now have ten years' worth of accrued interest instead of a dusty old pile of games that, compared to today's technology, look as if someone rendered them with a box of crayons. When you have goals and spend time thinking good thoughts about those goals, you are naturally going to behave in a way that is more beneficial to your future.

In the following scenario, we have an accurate analysis of the past and present. If you do not make any changes in the present, this becomes an accurate prediction of the future.

If you are in the 98 percent group, this is your final destination. Remember the list: Out of one hundred people who start working at the age of twenty-five, by the age sixty-five:

1 is wealthy
4 have adequate capital in savings for retirement
3 are still in the workforce
63 are dependent on Social Security, friends, relatives, or charity
29 are dead.

The average savings of a fifty-year-old in the U.S. is $2500. There are currently thirty two million Americans threatened with economic failure or bankruptcy. More than one million Americans filed for bankruptcy in the year 2000. Out of every one hundred Americans who reach the retirement age of sixty-five, sixty-two retire with less than $25,000 in assets and depend on Social Security or family for their retirements. Another thirty-five retire with less than $100,000 in assets and some form of pension in addition to Social Security and are just making it in their retirement. Two of the three remaining retirees have an adequate pension or retirement account. They have assets of between $100,000 and $750,000. *Only one is financially independent.*

You can greatly change your future by changing your present. To change your present you need to understand and learn operant conditioning and the law of attraction. You do not have to understand the fundamental universal laws of physics. Most of the people do not know how the law of gravity works but we can make highly accurate predictions, whether we took the time to learn modern physics or not.

A small percentage of the population has a fear of flying. The *past* shows airplanes do fall out of the sky. In the *present*, if you stay away from flying in an airplane, a very highly accurate prediction is that you will not die in one *(future)*.

The results are the same with the law of attraction, whether you understand it or not. Negative thoughts *create* negative actions and Positive thoughts *create* positive actions. It is safe to say a large majority of the population is in a negative-*creates*-negative mode by default.

Once you have used the law of attraction to obtain positive results, you merely need to keep on going, using a process called operant conditioning. The principles behind this process will be detailed in Chapter 5.

While you are learning to generate positive thoughts in order to affect outcomes in your life, keep in mind the importance of perseverance. Perseverance is formed through an ongoing continual assessment of emotional neurological biochemical processes, produced again and again by the hypothalamus and closely monitored by a series of checks and balances through the belief system of the individual.

It takes an enormous amount of perseverance and determination and an ongoing production of neurological chemical reactions to produce a short- or long-term positive outcome. This outcome may be an individual's completing a doctoral or medical degree, or the production of a life-long contribution like the theory of relativity, or, more recently, the invention of turning hydrogen into fuel to power the space shuttles.

3.7 Perseverance at a Neurological Biochemical Level

If you ask a psychologist what perseverance is, the short answer may be the relentless repetitive pursuit of a desired behavior or outcome. It is a commonly situational response. At a superficial level, this explanation suffices. However, it is critical to understand this process at a neurological biochemical level.

The most important key factor is to understand the law of attraction and how it relates to what is happening internally. In order to take advantage of the law of attraction, you are going to need to carefully maintain this internal environment, keeping it positive by persevering. How can you achieve this perseverance in your own life? What reminders can you use to help yourself stay on track?

At a superficial level, we target a goal and the mind starts the process of achieving it. Success is always determined by how the goal was perceived, just as in the example of a man eyeing a beautiful woman at a party. The outcome is based on your perception. If you persevere in generating positive thoughts, you will reach your personal and financial goals more quickly and more easily.

The speed of the process remains within the control of the individual's personality. The achievement of all goals is a direct result of and under control of long-term biochemical connections within billions of neurological tissues that form each person's belief system. It has nothing to do with intelligence quotient (IQ). This is where perseverance comes in, a process where an achievement is the result of a relentless pursuit to acquire the desired goal. The goal can and will be attained because the thinking, creative process will find the way to convert it into reality.

One of the most celebrated scientists of all time did not pass the admittance test to the university on his first attempt; he had to return to finish high school. The history of modern physics describes Einstein as a relentlessly persistent individual. The results of this personality trait are well documented in history.

Some of these complicated successful achievements do not just happen on the first attempt. They are the products of thought patterns and ideas that happen over and over until results are achieved. Perseverance plays an important role.

Astronaut, famous rock star, famous writer, millionaire: these a few of the choices a ten-year-old might give you when asked what he wants to be when he grows up. The average adult may consider some of these choices unattainable goals. It is clear not everyone becomes an astronaut or a rock star, but those that do believe it is possible achieve it. The lack of perseverance shows up in the large percentage of unsuccessful individuals in our population.

What makes the personality patterns of a ten-year-old change so drastically as he grows older? The primary factor of change is the law of the attraction. It seems as we grow older, the people who tell us to go ahead, it can be done, you can be whatever you want to be are the same people who later tell us not to try that, it is too hard, it is not going to happen, or you are not smart enough. They have good intentions, but are not aware they are conditioning the person to settle for less. Most likely, they experienced the same conditioning with their parents. It is as infectious as a viral flu.

If you change your belief system to be more positive, you will be ready to make the law of attraction work for you. Once your improved belief system prompts the continual creation of positive thoughts, it's only a matter of time before you reach your goals.

Surround yourself with mediocrity and you will be a part of the group. However, surround yourself with success and surprisingly, success comes your way. If you are in an unsuccessful environment for several years, you can easily be conditioned to that state of mind. You can sit in a dead-end situation for years unless you change your mentality.

A good example of an unsuccessful environment can often be found in an office setting. In some offices, the decor is drab, the air conditioner runs too much or not enough, the boss is unreasonable, and every worker in the place has learned that it feels better to complain and get sympathy from one another than to work to make the venture more successful—even though this ultimately harms their own individual careers. While everyone shivers under gusty vents in their gray cubicles, muttering complaints about how unfair it is that they are expected to finish a ten-page memo before quitting time, they miss opportunities to develop new skills, organize efforts to petition for the improvement of their office at the next board meeting, and form other strategies that might improve the situation.

Sure, the initial environment isn't these workers' fault. But their reaction to it is what sets them up for perpetual failure. Ironically, their distaste for their environment is the very thing that will trap them in it.

The law states you will always attract (create) the things you think about, and if you think of all the ways you cannot achieve your goal, it will never ever happen. Your mind will not work toward the goal because unconsciously you are convincing yourself you will *never* achieve it, and the more you focus on the negative the more negative thoughts you will create. It's not an internal voice talking to you and certainly not an imaginary person inside your head. It is all a process of neurological biochemical by design.

3.8 The Biochemical Dead End

The average individual is bombarded constantly by the media with marketing campaigns. You're told you have to thinner, you have to be beautiful, you have to buy the best house or the best car, you have to be the most intelligent. The ideals and situational goals that everyone is struggling to become are, in reality, mostly unattainable goals. This mindset is part of the illusion that everyone is trying to achieve by cleverly designed media marketing strategies. It causes you to displace your focus, setting your personality in time out, and leaving you exhausted, living your life in mediocrity by lowering your standards in order to become complacent and conditioned with what you have.

For instance, exercise is scientifically documented to result in physical benefits. Excluding those with serious physical conditions or other rare limitations, everyone benefits from exercise—no matter their body type. This is a scientific fact; it is undeniable. If a woman is trying to get in shape, she can choose to focus on this truth, building it into her belief system and using her faith in this truth to create positive thoughts.

Alternatively, she can instead focus on the impossible, photo-shopped beauty she sees on magazine covers and decide that working out will get her washboard abs and tiny thighs, just like she sees on the model. If this is her expectation, a failure to see such results will soon cause her to become conditioned to failure as she thinks, *This isn't going to work anyway*, or *I've been working out for two months, and I still haven't gotten much thinner.*

That woman will give up once she fails to see the results she expected and begins generating negative thoughts as a result of her disappointment. Meanwhile, the woman who believes that exercise has health benefits regardless of someone's size or shape can continue to work out—and perhaps, after a long while, even attain the washboard abs and tiny thighs that the other woman missed out on.

You stop competing because the negative conditioning is overwhelming. This causes the creative process to go on stand-by when you could be using that associative region of the brain to create success and increase your standard of life. This conditioning leaves people sinking lower and lower as the time passes.

Unfortunately, this is exactly what happens when you vacate the associative regions of your personality; you are setting aside all of your attempts at success, leaving self-doubt and questioning: *What am I? Why am I here? Is there any purpose to my life? What direction am I taking? Who disconnected the power to my belief system? My life is falling apart.* All of this leads to the biochemical dead end.

What happens when you turn off the power to the belief system? *I cannot be that thin. I cannot buy that house. I will not be able to achieve that. I am not smart enough. I do not have time to go back to school. I do not have enough money. I will not be able to compete. I am not that beautiful. I do not have enough time.* These types of responses happen once you start bouncing unattainable thoughts into the internal belief system. What is not self-serving goes right into the brain's recycling bin.

This is why it is critical to give the proper shape to a thought process and create it with precision. We cannot manifest the thought unless it goes through the proper belief filter as it pertains to the operational personality system.

The next time you are trying to manifest a thought into reality, grab the lamp, rub it, and wait for the genie—he will grant your wish. Try asking your belief system if that works. Your personality will pick up the phone and call the shrink. The lamp genie is an excellent metaphor, but the genie is you. You are the architect of your own reality.

Every human on the planet has the belief that he or she is the architect of his or her own reality. All we have to do is relate to it and understand how it works. It's not an easy task at first but, we can all remember how difficult the multiplication tables were to learn and some of us with advanced degrees can remember the difficulty of learning organic chemistry, but if you passed the class, the information is in your database.

3.9 Who is the Architect of Your Reality?

All individuals at one time or another—even those whose problems seem to be reoccurring and overwhelming—have worked very hard to improve their situations. Countless of times, they fail to succeed in anything they do. They often seem to be in a state of constant financial distress and confusion. Over the years, they have asked themselves, "Why is it nothing works for me?" The initial answer to this question is unique to each individual, but the most important thing to understand is that we are the architects of our own reality. Reality is the result of the manifestation or construction of ideas and thoughts that originate as a neurological biochemical process in the brain and end up in the creative associative regions. These neuronal nets make your thoughts or ideas come to life. When we are in the process of creation, we all operate under the same law and the same power; everyone shares the same neurological design and brain structures. We are all built the same when it comes to the physical construction of the brain; where we differ is in the construction of the ongoing building of billions of neurological connections to form these associative and processing regions. This is a process that originates from the time we are born and continues to the time of death.

What does that mean? All of us start out with the same computer; the difference is in the programming. We are in competition with ourselves and with others to constantly improve the program. However, some individuals seem to work more effectively than others toward defining and eventually achieving their goals.

Tell someone you are very successful, and the questions fly: "What do you do?"

"Where do you get your ideas?" "How did you start?"

Then, before you have a chance to answer even the first question, the inquirer will make a statement attributing your success to luck. "You know, I have always wanted to be very successful myself, but I have never had any type of luck in my life."

Fortunately, though, many individuals learn these processes and become marginally successful. Some become successful beyond their wildest imaginations, and most are not aware of the mechanics of what they have mastered.

Get a group of experts in a room and they may start by discussing theory and process, and before long the topic goes beyond what the average person can understand. Eventually, everyone tries to understand the law of attraction with the information within his or her own belief system. And if you do not believe in the supernatural, magical forces, **Karma**, universal energy, or the law of vibration, and if you are not religious, you can miss out on this great opportunity to learn how all of this can work for you.

The fact that you are reading this book says a lot about your need to change or create a major shift in your life. It is a good bet that you are at that critical crossroads in life, where you see just a few individuals becoming successful while you seem to just barely get by in wealth and relationships. Most individuals suffer in silence, wondering where their piece of the pie is. Go back and read again about the 98 percent group. This will tell you in which direction you are heading.

Have you ever seen how some individuals seem to turn everything they touch into gold and said to yourself, "I could have done that"? We all have experiences, stories, and incidents in which we see other people who seem to get more than their share and always seem to be in the right side of business ventures, experiencing financial success. We observe in amazement because whether it is one incident or a long-term situation, they are constantly in the creative process and in the success mode.

We all have the ability to be successful. As any financially successful individual will tell you, in addition to an individual particular way of thinking, you must possess equal amounts of persistence and determination. It is one thing to think you are going to be successful and apply the law of attraction; it is quite another to be able to manifest your thoughts and ideas into reality.

The process will involve operant behavioral conditioning (discussed at length in Chapter 5), and a relentless perseverance with no other thoughts but those goals in mind. This will allow your brain to activate the creative process within you. Are you up to this challenge? If your answer is yes, then by all means, let us get started.

3.10 Powerfully Positive Thinking

Many people, including some of your own friends and relatives, entertain the fantasy of becoming very successful one day. We place successful individuals on high pedestals. We have come to picture them as unique, very intelligent with special talents, or driven by greed and having better opportunities than the rest of us. Nothing is further from the truth; a large percentage do not even know how they fell into wealth. They were simply tapping into their own resources and making thoughts become things.

Let us jump into a time machine and go back to the year 1980 to meet up with Bill Gates when he was twenty-five years old. Tell him you came from the future to advise him by our calendar year of 2009 he is going to be one of the richest men in the world. Mr. Gates would most likely dismiss you as a crazy lunatic, but the truth is that he developed his operating system after many years of positive thoughts toward its creation. You can spot the same long-term positivity in any successful individual from any time in history.

It is also important to know many that individuals are driven to be successful and come up with ideas and thoughts that are moneymaking opportunities but fail because they lack perseverance. Too many individuals give up because they do not experience immediate results and never get beyond the first step in the process. They generally stop the process somewhere in the middle because they fail to understand a critical factor in the thought process; it takes a continuous effort and elimination of all interference to manifest an idea.

In building your reality, you must understand the process of interference, which is explained thoroughly in section 3.13.

Our body is created by our mind. It all begins in the cell; the cell is a protein-producing factory constantly receiving signals from the brain. All of the cells in our body are constantly multiplying. Cell structures are always modifying to accommodate biochemical changes. Modifications are often changes in sensitivity in receptors. If a given receptor or a given drug or internal juice is bombarded for a long period of time at a high intensity, it will shrink up the cell and cause the cell to be desensitized so that the same amount of drug or internal juice will elicit a much smaller response.

If these cell structures are bombarded with same attitude (jealousy, frustration, doubt, envy, despair, depression, sadness, shame, grief, fear, and guilt) or the same chemical over and over again on a daily basis, when the cell divides, that next cell will have more receptor sites for the emotion neurological peptides and less receptor sites for food exchange, creating deficits in the waste and toxins of the cell removal process.

This same bombardment of emotional neurological peptides also causes aging. All aging is a result of improper protein production. Aging is cause by the loss of elastin, a protein that plays an important part in keeping elasticity in the skin. Poor production of digestive enzymes causes poor digestion. Poor production of synovial fluid cause our bones to become brittle. All of this is due to improper protein production in the cells that have been in a chemical environment, taking years of emotional (jealousy, frustration, doubt, envy, despair, depression, sadness, shame, grief, fear, and guilt), chemical attacks. The cell modifies and adjusts receptors sites to accommodate the overwhelming production; this leaves the cell with biochemical emotional fatigue or the repetitive production of a specific peptide chain that can cause the biochemical emotional fatigue, which leads to more and more of the same. More negative emotions (jealousy, frustration, doubt, envy, despair, depression, sadness, shame, grief, fear, and guilt) create more negative emotions. Even though it may seem like it they are *attracting* , they are *creating*.

The good part about all of this is that it is never too late. No matter how severe your emotional state is, the biochemical productions can reverse and create a shift just by doing things that make you feel good. It does not happen overnight; it is a slow process, but it is completely and totally reversible.

3.11 A False Belief of Success

We are the smallest particle of the bigger whole we call society, and our entire population adheres to the same false belief of success. This might be an outrageous statement or not; you can decide for yourself. The inculcation process starts from the moment of birth and continues throughout your productive years. By the time you reach adolescence, you have been lulled by society into a distorted believe of success. You go to school, get your high school diploma, and hopefully find a trade. In order for you to achieve a higher degree of success, society encourages you to seek and complete further education to get a career. Upon completion, you are encouraged to work for a large corporation, get married, purchase a home, have 2.5 children, plan your retirement, work for forty to fifty years, retire, and live happily ever after.

This is the great American dream, and if you bought into it, you have been set up to fail. Go back and check out the statistics I asked you to mark with a yellow marker. The great American dreamer retires happily ever after, with less than $2500 in the bank.

Not to mention the constant never-ending struggle to abide by this false belief. Staying inside these parameters is a magical act, and if by any chance you do not follow society's parameters, if you deviate from the norm or don't follow the acceptable societal path, you are made to feel you have failed—by your friends, family, or co-workers, the media, and society. In fact, statistics show that only 1 percent—one out of one hundred individuals—retire to live a comfortable financial life. Was the first comment outrageous or not?

3.12 The Formation of Reality

We take for granted many aspects of reality. To understand reality, we must first understand how we acquire the notion of reality. From the start of our lives, we begin to formulate our concept of what is real. This concept always follows the same universal laws. We cannot have reality without the mind entering into it. What we call "the mind" happens to be an immense neurological biochemical system with billions of connections that form and becomes our interpreter of how we see the world around us. Information comes in as visual cues through the eyes for processing in the occipital lobes, where the information is processed as neurological biochemical reactions for storage in the associative regions of the brain. Every process follows the same scientific and universal law. Where it differs, is in the perception process; this is where individuality takes over and reality becomes unique to the individual.

It all comes down to one set of universal laws, and these laws apply to everyone in the same manner without any exceptions. Reality becomes our own perceived notion of our environment.

One question that remains unexplained how the brain can see an object it has never coded into memory. An interesting example is the story of the Caribbean Indians who welcomed Columbus to the shores. The Indians were at first confused as to how the men came to their shores because they were not able to see the ships that brought them. They had never seen a ship before they had no visual coding of the ships. Once the tribal leader was able to see the ships on the horizon, his explanation and description of the ships to the rest of the tribe was the key to everyone's visualizing and coding into memory what they had not been able to see.

Once you involve the mind as the interpreter of reality, everything we see as individual interpreters is an illusion.

3.13 How Does Interference Work?

So much has been written on the fundamental facts of the law of attraction and the importance of the rule that like attracts like; the creation of positive thoughts so that you can attract positive results; positive and negative vibrations; positive and negative frequencies. The whole idea may seem a little out in space and perhaps even overwhelming. Do not be intimidated by the volume of information that is available. Understanding the neurological biochemical model will narrow it down to one theory, one science.

When you analyze all of the information from all disciplines, it all points to one major obstacle. Interference—the production of multiple neuropeptides that can cause a neutralization of one emotion and the development of another—is the killer of dreams. We all have a recycling bin, where all of our dreams and goals are stored and waiting to come alive. To reactivate your dreams and goals, you have to control the gatekeeper. Let me take you on a journey toward understanding the internal neurological biochemical process of interference and how it can bring you out of the dead end.

With a simple demonstration, I am going to show you how interference works in your brain. Take a sheet of paper and at the very top write the number $250,000. Now draw a line down the middle of the page and on the left side write as many ways you can think of to make $250,000; on the right side, write down all of the ways you will fail to make $250,000. The average person writes between three to five ways on the left side of the page, and ten to fifteen ways to fail on the right side of the paper. The fact is that if you wrote anything on the right side of the page, you would never, ever, ever make $250,000. Whatever information you wrote on the right side will always cause interference in your mind and always interfere with your making that amount of money. The right side of the paper needs to be blank in order for you to search for ways to make that amount of money. The slightest bit of interference causes the creativity to come to a complete stop. The fact that individuals write down more ways to fail than to succeed indicates the state of mind of the average individual.

Every bit of information you are processing is headed in the direction of creating and manifesting your reality. The mind does not know the difference between success and failure. The moment you bring up a thought of failure, the gatekeeper diverts the information and does a U-turn right into the brain's recycle bin; there it will sit with all of the other dreams and unaccomplished goals waiting for reactivation.

The thought and its content becomes useless; always remember, making $250,000 is a combination of thoughts and ideas you are creating in order to make it come into your reality.

Go back to recent inventions. The operating system in your computer was at one time a thought with a set of ideas, and someone became a multibillionaire when those thoughts manifested into reality.

I am sitting here writing this book at a popular bookstore, drinking a cup of coffee. The cup has a sleeve to protect my fingers from burning. Remember Jay Sorensen the inventor of that sleeve (as discussed in section 1.2)? When he decided to explore the possibility of manufacturing such a product, he followed these two key steps:

1. Avoid telling anyone. When you have an idea, do not tell a soul. Even people close to you will try to convince you that your idea is idiotic. If you wake up the gatekeeper that is interference, your potential fortune will be up for grabs by the next idiot who feels like laughing all the way to the bank.

2. File a patent for the invention. In other words, believe in your future success. If you don't believe in your ability to manufacture and sell a product, you're unlikely to take such a step, which will impede a future successful outcome. Don't wait to have a popular product—patent it first.

Have you had any good ideas lately?

CHAPTER 4
The Biology of Belief

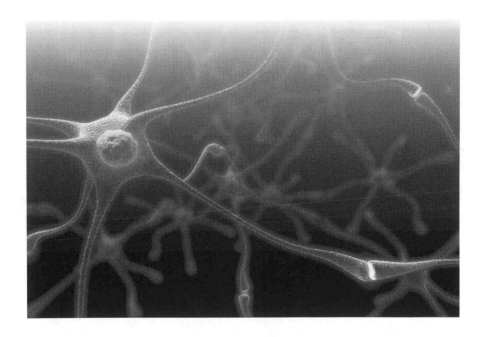

4.1 First, a Warning

Financial consultants and experts are forecasting very difficult financial times ahead because of the lack of successful avenues available to the average individual at this moment in time. Unemployment, real estate, mortgages, foreclosures, and bankruptcies indicate critical economic hardships for 98 percent of the population. In this type of environment, success becomes very difficult to achieve at any level. When is the last time you heard a good investment idea—not a get-rich-quick schemes that scams or takes advantage of consumers?

The answer to survival in this horrific financial situation is simple psychological behavioral conditioning. I will take a brief moment to explain how we got into this mess and how to get out.

If you have read this far, you are well aware you can condition anyone to do pretty much anything you want. We are all aware we have been conditioned to live in a false state of success. The average American is currently living from paycheck to paycheck and always looking at bankruptcy as an alternative. The ones not making it, along with the popular millionaire next door, file bankruptcy to wipe the slate clean. For those that do not know how that works, it is a simple task of legally passing the losses to the entity that lent you the money. It legally releases you from paying back the money you borrowed. So, if the entity was irresponsible and lent you money without collateral, it is destined to take the loss. The loss is then passed back to you in higher costs and it becomes a catch-22 until the bubble bursts—the bubble is bursting now.

If you carefully follow the gurus of the economy, you will discover they all are skeptical and pessimistic. For instance, John Hussman, an economic guru, wrote on February 14, 2010, that he has a couple main concerns, including unemployment and a second wave of credit losses, and says his economic outlook is "cautiously pessimistic." He believes last month's drop in the unemployment rate to be an anomaly, and he expects the jobless rate to peak in the 11- to 12-percent range.[10] All it is going to take to derail this economy is one small government incident and brace yourself for the worse financial crisis in history.

We are sitting in the eye of the hurricane. If the financial climate does not improve at the most basic, smallest level—the individual—the dollar will continue to decline. In fact, according to a January 26, 2009, article on the *History News Network*, "the amount of money printed in the past few months since the October economic crisis, has been absolutely unprecedented in U.S. history."[11] Is our government getting into the dangerous habit of printing more money to alleviate financial crises? If so, this could be devastating for the dollar. The value of real estate has decreased 45 percent. So where are we? We are sitting in the eye of the hurricane.

To improve things, change has to come from the bottom, not the top. The human creative processes all play a part and are a direct result of this neurological biochemical process. If you have been conditioned to stand by in failure mode because of how bad the situation is, the situation is not going to get any better.

The solution is simple. We all fabricate the same chemical neurological peptides structures and produce the same neurological transmitters in our neurological logical systems. Major critical shifts in your life can be produced by understanding how this all works and how it applies to you. It is time to let science help you change your reality.

At this time, it is safe to give you a brief warning. I predict three things will happen. First, some readers may not understand this information right away and it may take multiple readings of this book to grasp the concepts to reprogram thought patterns. Second, you may understand the concepts and have difficulty putting them into practice, because you have been conditioned for so many years to have these negative emotional thought patterns. Third, you may be one of those individuals that have been conditioned to over-evaluate and think of ways this will not work for you, which is also a big part of the conditioning effect of negative emotional production, stifling creativity and grinding it to a halt. Either way, it is something that does not require much intelligence or scientific knowledge. It is not difficult and everyone can put it to work. The only effort on your part will be learning this knowledge; it involves very basic information of ongoing neurological procedures that are constantly happening in your body as they relate to you and your internal motivational and creative forces. It does not require high levels of education or a high IQ. The knowledge is so basic I can safely say that learning multiplication tables is much harder.

4.2 One Theory, One Science

There have been many disciplines and individuals going around the world trying to explain the law of attraction. Unfortunately, that has done more harm than good. Let's say you could go back in time to visit a psychiatric hospital when the treatments of choice were the spinning chair, **copious** bloodletting, the removal of possibly infected viscera, the extraction of teeth, electric shock, forcible restraint for days or weeks, wrapping in cold blankets, inducing coma, causing backbreaking convulsions, slicing through the brain with an ice pick, drilling holes in the head, sterilization, and female genital mutilation.

Talk to the chief of staff and tell him those treatments are grotesque and inhumane; you know for a fact of medications that can completely control insanity. Educate him on our current research on **hallucinations** as neurological biochemical thoughts incorrectly routed because an overload of certain specific **neurotransmitters** that are released into this vast tissue composed of interconnected billions of cells called neurons that have axons extending throughout the entire nervous system. Quickly jump back in the time machine before they drill a hole in your head.

It is time to clear up the backwoods concept of the law of attraction and use proven current scientific research in operational neurological chemical functioning to explain the law of attraction. We are all in agreement on how the body functions and we just recently started to understand complex neurological biochemical processes that go on in the brain.

There should not be any controversy. It is one theory, one science. We have respected scientists, **metaphysicians**, philosophers, visionaries, psychologists, and medical doctors stating that we all work with one infinite power and we all operate under the same natural laws of the universe. The law of attraction works the same for all, indisputably.

My addition to the 98 percent solution of this critical problem is that we all operate under the same neurological biochemical processes and that is why anyone can apply the law if they understand it. You can be anything you want, you can have all the happiness you want, you can chose who you want to be, you can be more successful, you can be a millionaire, you can have the house of your dreams, you can create physical healing, and you can create mental healing. The proof is that in one case after the another, it all happen because these people were able to apply the law of attraction. It all depends on how well you adapt the thinking processes required to create change. In order to penetrate your belief system and not have you discard any of my information, I am going to define what the law really is. Even though the popular application is positive attracts positive and negative attracts negative, in reality, the law of attraction is the process of positive *creates* positive and negative *creates* negative. It may seem that you are attracting positive or negative, but you are not attracting it—you are creating it. The more positive emotions you create, the more positive results you will create.

4.3 Old Ideas, New Explanations

Advances in scientific biomedical research have given birth to a relatively much simpler explanation than the traditional, controversial interpretations. This model enables everyone to understand the mechanics of the law of attraction by eliminating the mystic, supernatural concepts and the overwhelmingly confusing theories proposed by any and all current disciplines, since these concepts limit the participants.

The law of attraction is the universal law that influences all emotional neurological biochemical processes inside every individual, and, perhaps most important, gives the individual a clear explanation and understanding to pursue the success and happiness it can provide to anyone who learns the concept. It is not an **autonomous response**; if you do not learn how it works, you will not be able to put it into practice. In some cases, it may happen by accident, but the information you are reading is to give you full control and perform on demand in order to experience continuous results.

The modern technology that makes all of this possible is our newfound understanding of neurological biochemical brain functions, which explains the formation of thoughts and ideas in the associative regions of the brain.

Regardless of the explanation behind the law of attraction, virtually anyone can use the law of attraction if he or she learns how it works and how it is applied to everyday life. Don't stress if you find yourself struggling to grasp the more complex explanations of how the law of attraction works. While a basic biological understanding of the law of attraction will be helpful to you, what matters most is that the process of thinking positively in order to realize goals has been used by every successful individual in recorded history.

4.4 Neurological Biochemical Process of the Law of Attraction

Neurological biochemical research shows our thoughts play an important role in the manifestation of success, happiness, miracle medical cures, and overall aspects of creativity.

If you keep the system working ultimately to its highest operational capacity, tumors, viruses, outside invaders, and internal metabolic errors are eliminated. Medical research shows the immune system is greatly influenced by our thoughts. In a landmark study described in a 2003 article in the New York Times,[12] researchers at the University of Wisconsin reported that negative emotions can weaken our immune responses to a flu vaccine. "The brain has the capacity to modulate peripheral physiology," Dr. Richard J. Davidson was quoted as saying, "and it modulates it in ways that may be consequential for health."

All aspects of creativity work on the very same tangible thought processes and neurological biochemical pathways I will be discussing throughout this book. This information will create insight and awareness into your own internal resources in order to activate your thoughts in the direction of achieving success and fulfilling your dreams.

4.5 The Minifactory of Dreams

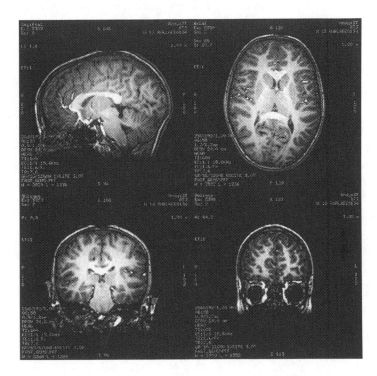

In section 3.1, "Attraction by Default," you learned that the hypothalamus produces different peptide chains in response to negative or positive thinking. Let's examine the biological processes of positive thinking a bit more closely.

The body is basically a carbon unit that manufactures twenty different amino acids all together to formulate its physical structure. The body is a protein-producing machine.

The hypothalamus is like a minifactory and the place that assembles certain chemicals that match every emotion we experience. Each emotion has a different biochemical sequence. These particular chemicals are called peptides; they are small chains of amino acid sequences. The hypothalamus produces and assembles these small chains of amino acids into certain neuronal peptides to match every emotional state we experience on a daily basis. There are peptide chains for anger and peptide chains for sadness, there are peptide chains for victimization, there are peptide chains for lust—there are peptide chains that match every emotional state.

After assembly, all of these peptide chains are released into the bloodstream. Once in the bloodstream the chains find their way to different centers or different targeted cells in the body. Every single cell in the body has corresponding receptors for every peptide chain on the outside—one cell can have millions of receptors studying its surfaces and opening up to the outside world. When a peptide chain docks on the surface, it is literally like a key going into a lock. Once attached to the receptor, it releases the neurological chemicals into the cell to perform the designated task.

Along the outside of these cells there are millions of receptor sites receiving incoming information. A peptide sitting attached to a receptor changes the cell in many ways. It sets off a series of internal biochemical events; some of them end up changing the actual nucleus of the cell. Each cell is definitely alive and each cell has a consciousness. It is safe to say the cell is the smallest unit of consciousness in the body.

4.6 Thinking in the Right Direction

How did we get here? This is a subject of much controversy and the center of ongoing debates. One group claims we were created and placed here on Earth by a higher supreme being in a very short time, and the other group claims we evolved through millions of years and developed from a one-cell organism.

We do not really know and probably never will, but there are some things we do know, whichever side is correct. We are in a constant effort to guide this sophisticated piece of creation in the right direction so that we can get the most out it.

Let me go over some important facts to get you acquainted. Simplicity is the mother of understanding, so I will put forth my middle-school biological explanation instead of the other, which has the tendency to lose some folks.

We are what scientists call a carbon unit, and that is because we are made up of a molecular structure composed of carbon and hydrogen molecules. We can now skip sixty chapters ahead and go into the nuts and bolts of the entire operation.

Let's begin with a quick inventory of what we have and go over some of the aspects of its construction.

We have a centralize command center (brain) that is constantly monitoring everything that goes on externally and internally. This command center is able to process *four hundred to five hundred million bits of information per second*. It has monitoring systems balancing and assimilating information from a complex set of senses; it has a system to convert neurological biochemical into thoughts and ideas in order to create its proper unique identity; it monitors motor centers for movement and maintenance centers to control internal heat and cold; it monitors checks and balances on any type of molecule chain created or produced by any of its organs. It has monitoring systems for reproduction and monitoring systems for hormonal balances. It has a superb system of protection (the immune system) against outside invasions of things that do not belong in the body and a demolition system to destroy defective things created by the body. There are also monitoring systems for food intake and food breakdown (stomach), centers to assimilate the food breakdown (intestines), centers for the production of energy (liver) and for storing energy (fat tissue), and efficient centers for waste removal. This command center controls the pump (heart) and the pumping of liquids that carry nourishment to every cell and another system to remove waste products of this operation. It is overall a very sophisticated, amazing piece of machinery.

We are going to narrow down our focus to a very important section, and that is the production of neurological biochemical and how these form thoughts and ideas to form personality. We will see how every chemical reaction is involved in the creative and motivational process and how we can create internal changes that can improve greatly our external functional world, which we call our reality. Internal changes are comprised of thoughts. All thoughts have an process of neurobiochemical production. The internal will shape and manifest the external. It all depends on the perseverance and rehearsal and the lack of interference in the thought process.

Now that you know the internal mechanism, your task will be to create thoughts of the things you want. You can write them in a notebook or on a piece of paper, you can cut them out of a catalog and post them where you can see them everyday, you record them and listen to them over and over and find a way to view the goals in multiple settings, or you can take pictures, but they have to be things that you want and they have to be precise and clear. The major point is they have to be *precise and clear*. The thoughts you are creating cannot be global; they have to be specific and you have to write down specific instructions for achieving them.

For instance, perhaps you have been working in a corporate job that does not feel very morally rewarding. Perhaps you are interested in working for charities and making a positive difference in the world. It's one thing to say, "I plan to become a freelance grant writer who works at home." It's quite another to actually write out the steps required. Where will you get your grant-writing certificate? What sorts of nonprofit organizations do you intend to work for? How many grant requests do you plan to write a month? What is your target annual income? Provide as much information as you can for each goal that you have.

You are going to direct one thing at a time that you want to come into your existence. Everything that is going to come into your existence will be attracted (created) by you. At this time, do not worry about how they are going to materialize. Your thoughts will start the construction process. The images of all those things you want will be stored in your mind and, surprisingly, construction will begin once you are thinking about them over and over.

This law is available to all, but only a small percentage actually know, practice, or have any knowledge of its workings. The statistics are staggering: 98 percent of the population is not aware of anything we are discussing. It is frightening to think our economy and our society is designed like this by default.

Every thought and its contents will be the blueprint of what you want to be created into your existence. In this creative process if you devote time to thinking of anything you do *not* want, it will continue to happen, because you are creating the thoughts of that particular situation you do *not* want. Your surrounding world is responding to your thoughts and you will get more of what you do *not* want. Lets make sure we understand this. If you are thinking about something you do *not* want and you spend precious biochemical to push that situation away, the result will be that you are *not* pushing it away but bringing it into your existence.

The creative process is an ongoing biochemical process, so when you are having a thought or a series of thoughts, you are actually formulating and constructing your outside world.

If you formulate an outline of the *bad* things that are currently happening to you, the biochemical process you are creating is a direct focus of how *bad* things are. You will continue to feel lousy and by default will continue to have bad things attracted (created) to you. You cannot focus on things you do *not* want. By default, your biochemical process will continue to make you feel *bad* and there will not be any situational shift. *Bad will bring more bad.* Focus on good situations and you produce good results. The mind will shape the thoughts of your perception. It is time-dependent; your results will not manifest overnight or immediately. It may take some time, but the process of getting there will feel great. There are only two factors that help you navigate through all of this process.

The first factor is positivity. As you have learned, specific *positive emotions* exist: pride, desire, gratitude, hope, empathy, happiness, euphoria and joy. The helpful biochemicals are created with pride, desire, gratitude, hope, empathy, happiness, euphoria, and joy and the progress-inhibiting emotional biochemicals are created by jealousy, frustration, doubt, envy, despair, depression, sadness, shame, grief, fear, and guilt.

If you are producing feel-bad emotional biochemicals and what you are doing feels bad to you, immediately stop that thought or the series of thought processes—you are going in the wrong direction. So when you are creating that feel-good biochemical process, your navigator is saying to you, "That is what we need; lets produce some more." These good thoughts will formulate your future experience.

You can create a feel-good peptide by creating a thought that you know will make you feel good (pride, desire, gratitude, hope, empathy, happiness, euphoria, or joy). To gain at least a general notion of where you want the thought to end up, in what part of the creative process, you need to rehearse and revisit the objectives the feel-good thoughts will create during the thinking process. If you have those thoughts—remember, you have to be very specific and precise—the end product happens through the process of rehearsal.

4.7 What is the Placebo Effect?

The neurological biochemical process of the placebo effect is perhaps the most interesting example I can provide to explain the biochemical effects of the law of attraction. Many studies have indicated that if we expect something to work, it will. This effect is not always mild or insignificant. In fact, sometimes, a sugar pill proves just as effective as an actual prescription, as long as the patient believes the sugar pill is real medicine.

The placebo effect plays a very important role in the pharmaceutical industry. It has become the cornerstone of all pharmaceutical manufacturers. Before drugs are introduced to consumers, they are required to go through stringent testing. An important part of the testing process requires drug manufactures to perform tests to rule out the placebo effect in order to determine whether the actual medication alleviated the medical condition or the individual alleviated the medical condition with his thought process. Consumer protection guidelines require every drug before it reaches the consumer to be tested for physical and psychological efficacy.

One area where the placebo effect has generated controversy is in the treatment of depression (which, of course, is characterized at least in part by negative thoughts). Amazingly, despite the fact that antidepressant medication is so routinely described, it has never been proven to be significantly more effective than a sugar pill in any but the most severe cases of depression, as a 2010 *Newsweek* article points out.[13].Yet antidepressants help three-quarters of the people who take them. If antidepressants are "basically expensive Tic Tacs," as the article noted, why are they so effective? Simply put, their effectiveness relies on "the holy trinity of belief, expectation, and hope," to the extent that physicians are afraid their patients will find out about the placebo effect and lower their expectations, thus reducing positive outcomes.

You read that right: physicians have so much respect for the power of positive thinking that they don't want their patients to find out that the law of attraction is helping them—just in case those patients don't believe that the law of attraction really works. As it turns out, as a universal law, the law of attraction applies to everyone, whether they believe in it or not.

Since drug manufacturing is also a multibillion dollar business, every drug manufacturer directs a large amount of research into finding a cure for the common cold. Large drug manufacturers often conduct drug trials to investigate the efficacy of new cold remedies. These trials consist of administering the medicine to two separate groups of individuals with flu symptoms. They give the new medication to one group and a sugar pill to the other. Every person in both groups is under the belief they are taking the real medication. The results of such drug trials will often even amaze researchers. If the medication works, they find a significant percentage of the group that took the real medication improving their flu condition and symptoms, but they also find a significant number of individuals who took the sugar pill showing remarkable improvement when compared with a group that took nothing at all.

4.8 An Explanation of the Common Cold

If the individuals in the control group create specific repeated thoughts and are convinced their cold remedy (in this case, a sugar pill) works, their improvement is under the direct influence of the law of attraction. I will precede my explanation with a brief explanation of the common cold. The average common cold has a life expectancy of five to seven days—from the time the first viral germ comes in through the mucous membranes and reproduces billions of times until the time the last germs is destroyed by an immune system T-killer cells. The average individual already has a built-in system to fight it, so when the viral infection is detected by the body, the immune system kicks into overdrive and starts to manufacture T-killer cells. It then becomes a numbers game. The major objective is to overthrow the invader.

The unresolved problem with this situation is that the immune system is not always operating at optimal levels because there are too many environmental situations constantly depleting the immune system. The other problem is that viral germs duplicate much faster than the immune system can fabricate T-killer cells, or the soldiers, to combat the cold or flu. It literally takes about five to seven days for the immune system to catch up and eliminate the invader. It is a well-known fact that we do not yet have a cure for the common cold. The reason is that all viral infections have an exceptional mechanism of protection.

They can live in the external and the internal world, and in both situations they can mutate and take on different identities. By the time you get it and it is passed on to five other individuals, the identity has changed. This is the reason medical research has not found one cure-all vaccine, so we are left only with two types of medications, one that can raise the immune system and one to relieve symptoms.

4.9 The Law of Attraction and Medicine

The fact that the cold will be eliminated in an individual who has a strong belief the medication will work is a perfect example of internally created thoughts creating results. If you are creating the thoughts and your belief system is convinced of the end results, the immune system will activate in the following manner: The neurological biological chemistry will produce a constant release of neurological peptide chains released from the hypothalamus into the bloodstream to the targeted cells of the immune system. The immune system fights all outside infections by producing T-killer cells; when you are experiencing a cold, your immune system is producing T-killer cells at a much slower rate compared to the faster duplication of the viral infection germ. If you increase the immune system to step up the production of T-killer cells to the point of saturation, the macrophage process destroys the viral invader and the flu symptoms stop.

In this case, the law of attraction is so powerful that an individual can create a desired result by the simple process of creating thoughts, believing they will work, and activating other complex biochemical reactions to increase immune system functioning.

4.10 Creating Your Own Placebo Effect

By producing thoughts, we can induce a placebo effect by simply creating thought patterns that can penetrate the belief system of an individual and create phenomenal results. This is a process in complete control of the individual without any other aids. All it takes is to have the individual believe the information to be true and the internal biochemical changes shift in any desired direction. Early in my practice as a neuropsychologist, a married twenty-six-year-old patient was referred to me with a severe case of impotence. After a complete medical analysis to rule out a physical problem, I found the problem to be totally psychological without any physical pathology. I weighed the ethical implications of my plan of action and concluded that my plan would cause him no harm, and might just cure his affliction. The patient had been suffering with this condition for almost a year; his marriage was failing and he was showing signs of depression. He needed help, but I knew the solution would be much simpler than he'd ever expected.

I had one session with him and a separate session with the spouse. I explained to her that success of the treatment was dependent on her keeping the procedure confidential; in other words, if she disclosed what I was going to do, the treatment would fail. I told the patient I had come across information on a newly developed drug and research showed the drug to be very successful in treating impotence in Europe. I told him I thought he would be an excellent candidate for the treatment, which consisted of three injections, one every twenty-four hours. Studies showed excellent results by the second injection, and by the third injection all of the patients in the study were cured. I gave him three shots of saline solution. In those times we carried beepers. I received a 911 call on my beeper from his wife early Sunday thanking me and telling me they'd had sexual intercourse all night.

Let us examine what happened biochemically. The patient came to me with acquired thoughts and ideas in his belief system affecting his sexual performance. Performance anxiety is a major cause of impotence; in a vicious downward spiral, the more patients worry about whether a random incidence of impotence would repeat itself, the more likely they are to find themselves unable to perform. This downward spiral was likely responsible for my client's difficulties.

The patient was evasive and not a good candidate for psychotherapy. It takes many psychotherapy sessions for an impotent client to feel comfortable talking about the dysfunction, and in many cases, there are financial situations that preclude the patient's spending weeks of therapy because of the cost involved. This might have been a reason the process needed to resolved. My assessment was that he was in denial because he kept shifting the blame to his wife.

I implanted a thought solution and gave him the tools he needed to create his own proper thoughts to create a physical change. The success of the treatment came from his belief system. His thought patterns and his own personality neurological net made it come to reality. I spaced the injections over a period of three days to make sure he had plenty of time to work out his solution. This reinforces the power of the thinking process and how thoughts can influence any physical state.

4.11 The Law of Attraction and Miracle Medical Cures

When is the last time you heard about a medical miracle? A similar process to the placebo effect applies to those individuals that experience miraculous medical recoveries. According to *The Power of Positive Thinking*, by Dr. Norman Vincent Peale, medical science has well-documented cases of individuals' having malignant tumors disappear without any of the traditional modes of therapy and miracle cures of individuals with chronic diseases not expected to live.

Just recently I became involved with a group of patients with stage two and three cancer, offering my services in neuropsychology. You may find some of my observations to be quite surprising.

But first, in order to understand how these miraculous cures and recoveries work, let us clear up some of the medical misconceptions of cancer. When I first started with this group of cancer patients, I invited them and their families to a seminar. I opened up the seminar with one question: What is cancer? You would be surprised that I have yet to find one person who could give me the correct answer. If I asked twenty-five individuals, I would receive twenty-five different versions of "cancer is when the cells turn bad and grow into a tumor and if you do not take care of it, you die." I would go around the room and even those with medical knowledge and background repeated the wrong answer.

In order to understand how a person with stage two or three cancer is able to go into remission without any of the traditional therapies like chemotherapy or radiation, the first thing you need to know is that cancer is a malfunction of the immune system. Second, the body is composed of over ten trillion cells, and every cell in your body is replaced within a period of time. Some cells, like blood cells, are replaced within hours, and some cells, such as hair cells, take several years. The human body is constantly reproducing cells. The ultimate goal is for every cell to produce an exact twin replica. This reproduction is far from perfect; a significant number of cells undergo mutation with metabolic errors and damaged duplicate sister cells.

A cell with damaged DNA can produce a cancerous cell or a cell with a new identity. The bad news is that inside your body this minute, you have a large number of damaged cells including cancer cells desperately trying to reproduce. The good news is the reason they do not reproduce is because the immune system has a unique first-line defense team of cells destroying any cells with a different identity. One group of this defense team goes around tagging for destruction anything not recognized as part of the body or with a different identity. The other part of the defense team group, the T-killer cells, find the tagged cells and destroy them by injecting the cell to destroy its content. Once the content is destroyed, the T-cells perform housekeeping and eat it. Individuals diagnosed with Acquired Immune Deficiency Syndrome, or AIDS, do not actually die of AIDS. They have a severe deficit of this line of defense, and if it is not treated aggressively, they die of an opportunistic disease such as cancer or pneumonia.

You now have the scientific medical answer for how a large number of these of these miraculous recoveries work. I knew that my success with the cancer patients would depend on my ability to build up their immune systems. In the case of stage three cancer in particular, cells have broken off the primary tumor and are floating in the bloodstream. The immune system can use T-cells to destroy the malignant cells, but unless many more T-cells are produced, the bad cells will ultimately overwhelm the good ones. The immune system of a cancer patient is always deficient, so an aggressive attempt to build up the immune system is necessary.

In a period of one year, I was able to put in remission twenty-seven out of twenty-eight patients. I was able to keep these patients with us because of two major contributions. First, I found a product in the Physicians Desk Reference book that was discovered over fifty years ago and recently perfected. The product is a protein molecule called **transfer factor.** Forty-eight hours after it is ingested, it raises the immune system 458 percent from its baseline.[14]

My success wasn't entirely based on pharmaceuticals, however. I knew that taking advantage of the law of attraction would be just as crucial. Because the immune system's functioning is strongly influenced by thought processes, I needed my patients to create positive thoughts in order to allow the medication to achieve its full potency.

To achieve my objective and create what some people call a miraculous medical cure, I would need patients that would understand they would be cancer-free within a short time and believe beyond a shadow of a doubt that the modality worked. Easier said than done—that became my main obstacle. We all understand now it is a numbers game. You need a huge production of T-killer cells to combat the cancer cells and win the battle to the point that it cannot be detected in the bloodstream, which is the medical description of a patient in remission.

Out of all the patients, I think I had one patient that was marginally convinced this process would work. The rest had nothing to lose and were willing but somewhat skeptical. I realized I would have to perform aggressive operant conditioning to achieve remission.

First I gave them transfer-factor research studies of patients in remission from New York University and Stanford University. I found literature on several medical doctors who'd had significant success in keeping patients in remission.

I bombarded each patient with transfer factor; they each took two capsules every four hours. I waited for laboratory results from each patient. I found that within ninety days, all but one patient had normal labs. Within one year, I had twenty-seven patients in remission.

I received calls from every patient's oncologist; they all wanted to know about the treatment modality. A couple doctors were so amazed with the results they stopped by my office for more in-depth information on the treatment.

You know where all of this is going? Was it a miracle medical cure? Or was a combination of the law of attraction working with transfer factor to speed up the immune system?

At times, some less scrupulous corporations might base their claims on the placebo effect. You can Google yourself a miracle cure for just about any ailment under sun. Unfortunately, the Internet has gotten so huge there is no way to police everyone selling his or her miracle cure or remedy. Beware even of some of the large multimillion dollar products marketed and supervised very closely by legal departments to stay inside the guidelines of consumer fraud.

I had an interesting experience several years ago. I was approached by a popular company selling a product through network marketing. They were looking for doctors to endorse their product. I was asked to speak at one of their seminars. They were holding several seminars weekly and attracting over five hundred individuals per seminar. Before getting involved, I requested information on their research and found very little mention of the placebo effect.

The product consisted of a blend of fruits with one special exotic fruit at the top of the list. We all know that fruits are full vitamins, antioxidants, and important nutrients, but my expectations of this fruit's medicinal value fell short of theirs. However, out of curiosity, I asked to attend the following meeting to know more about the product. I walked into a room, which could easily accommodate one thousand people, and it was packed, standing room only with people standing in the hallways. The presentation started with a short video followed by three speakers. The first one spoke about the product, the second talked about how to make money through network marketing, and the third closed the meeting by having those consuming the product testify how it cured their ailments.

The first testimonial was delivered by a gentlemen claiming that he had been sick with frequent colds for six months; thirty days after he'd been introduced to the product, he was cold-free and had even stopped taking antibiotics. The next was a lady with high blood sugar. She was introduced to the product and in sixty days later her blood sugar was under control. The next was a young man suffering from migraines; he was introduced to the product and in less than one week his migraines disappeared. The last one was a lady with irritable bowel syndrome. She claimed that forty-five days after she was introduced to the product, the condition had become manageable enough for her to be able to leave her house without any fear of "going in her pants."

From my analysis, there was no medicinal value in the product to cause any of these miracle cures. The most interesting part was that at the end of the meeting, one third of the room rushed to the front to join.

Aside from the individual with high blood sugar, I do not believe for one moment those people were lying about their healing. They were all operating under the influence of the law of attraction and the placebo effect. The same results could have been achieved with a bottle of sugar pills, much cheaper than the expensive bottle of juice. The power of thought can have remarkable and amazing results. We have an amazing human body with a remarkable system of protection against our outside and internal environment.

CHAPTER 5
Make Success an Addiction

5.1 The Role of Personality in Habits and Addictions

An addiction is simply a compulsive need to ingest a substance or exhibit a behavior.

Essentially, an addiction is a habit. Learning about how addictions are formed will offer some helpful insights into the nature of habits, good and bad. If you become addicted to success, you will become driven to achieve consistent results again and again. How is this accomplished?

The blueprint for duplication, or continuing to produce the same results, is all grounded in understanding personality as the constant growth and building blocks of emerging personality patterns (also referred to as **holographic patterns**) stored in the part of the brain that defines who we are as our expression to the outside world or to the observer. This projection to the outside world starts from birth as an intangible complex set of thoughts, ideas, and classifications in constant growth, which then becomes our role as others see us in respect to our part of reality.

How do others perceive you? Would they say you are independent and motivated? Do they see you as a mature, neat, put-together person or as a messier, more creative child at heart? In what ways might you have to adjust your inner being and outward image in order to achieve your desired goals?

Most important, understanding the process as it happens at the neuronal level is the key to implementing a desired outcome. Your personality affects your ability to produce positive thoughts in a manner that will allow you to reap financial gains and other benefits from the law of attraction.

The tangible part of all of this originates as a neurological biochemical process. A neuronal net consisting of billions of axonal connections creates short- and long-term relationships, processing 300 to 400 millions bits of information per second and operating very much like a computer processing data. Research shows the neurological biological construction of a thought happens as the direct result of interpreting, integrating, formulating, assimilating, storing, and discarding information.

You can appreciate the complexity and efficiency of this process when analyzing a dangerous situation in which a quick, life-saving decision needs to be made. You are driving on the freeway and someone passes you at high speed; further up the road, you watch the driver lose control and go into a canal. You run to the site and all you see is the rear of the car as it sinks fast into the water. What are you going to do? There is only one decision that needs to be made immediately. Jump into the water and save the driver or watch the person die. If we had the ability to view that decision-making process under a microscope as it occurs, it would seem like a controlled nuclear explosion of information and data traveling throughout every structure and functioning part of the nervous system. The decision to jump into the water is the result of trillions of functions happening simultaneously. It is a self-serving process going through all of the belief filters to activate the motor cortex to jump into the water or stand by and watch the car sink.

The major role of any action has to do with the belief system constructed within this complex neuronal biochemical net of connections. This belief system dictates the type of action that a person will produce under a given set of circumstances. For instance, if you see a child about to run after a ball right into traffic and you are within arm's reach, you will immediately reach out and grab the child's arm to keep her from darting in front of a car, even if that child is a stranger. This reflects your belief that human life is sacred and must be preserved when possible; this belief exists in your neuronal net. In order to manifest a thought into reality, the information has to match previously formed personality behavior patterns. If you have been conditioned to fail, the creative portion of this part of your personality is always on stand-by.

Another key to understanding the mechanics of failure is to understand that when new information is evaluated and information does not match the belief system of the individual, the information is discarded. Or, if the individual does not know of a specific way to achieve a certain process, the desired action is evaluated as impossible and discarded as an option.

Just because you have not yet made an annual income that satisfies you, that doesn't mean that you can't. Opportunities surround you every day, but if you stick with your typical habits instead of reacting to and reaching for those opportunities, they will pass you by. Unfortunately, such a nonreaction is the default setting of human behavior. If you work to change this setting, you will be miles ahead of the competition.

Most individuals, when presented with an opportunity for success, will remain in the same neutral mode, not reacting and not creating any new neurological biochemical changes to establish new thoughts, ideas, or situations. The process of creation abruptly stops when that neutral mode prompts the individual to fail to take advantage of an opportunity. The individual then remains in a negative mode, unable to experience new situations that will in turn prepare changes to brain chemistry needed to activate new creativity.

Every professional or famous person previously mentioned agrees: a negative state of mind will continue to attract negative situations, and for simplicity, the word *attraction* can be substituted with the word *creation*. The law of attraction states negative *attracts* more negative and positive *attracts* more positive, when in reality and biochemically, negative *creates* more negative and positive *creates* more positive.

How can you develop a new belief system, changing your personality into one that fosters an addiction to success? The answer lies in the process of operant conditioning.

5.2 The Two Types of Conditioning

An addiction essentially amounts to an extreme case of conditioning. You will find it helpful to understand two types of conditioning: operant conditioning and behavioral conditioning. You can use these two types of conditioning to build your addiction to success.

5.2.1 Operant Conditioning

Operant conditioning is the use of *consequences* to modify the occurrence and form a *new behavior.* Operant conditioning is distinguished from **classical conditioning**, also called *respondent conditioning,* or *Pavlovian conditioning,* in that operant conditioning deals with the modification and creation of thoughts (positive thoughts). These thoughts (positive thoughts) operate on the environment and are maintained by its consequences (success). The positive thoughts find their way to the creative associative regions (unconscious), and the brain finds the way to manifest them. Once you manifest or achieve the positive thought, neurotransmitters are released to the pleasure centers, giving you a sense of accomplishment and making you feel good. A *conditioned reinforcement* has just automatically created a *conditioned reflex.* Remember— The Millionaire Mindset is a primary example of a conditioned reflex, while classical conditioning deals with the conditioning of behavioral responses that are elicited by *prior consequences.* Operant conditioning is elicited by *ongoing consequences.* This entire process is neurological biochemical and under the direct result of the law of attraction. Ongoing positive results are reinforced and create more ongoing positive results.

Operant conditioning is a simple process of stimulus, response, and reinforcement, better described in psychology as behavioral operant conditioning. You can be behaviorally conditioned to produce both success and failure.

This is how operant conditioning works:

1. You behave in a certain way.

2. Your behavior results in a positive or negative outcome. If the outcome is positive, your behavior has been reinforced. If the outcome is negative, your behavior has been punished.

3. You increase or decrease the behavior depending on the response, even if this continued behavior proves harmful in other ways.

A famous experiment in conditioning involved placing electrodes in the pleasure centers of a rat's brain to provide sexual stimulation when a lever is pressed, while at the same time, the rat is electrically shocked. Each time the rat presses the lever, the intensity of the shock increases, but the rat will continue to press the lever until it is electrocuted. All of this happens using the same neurological pathways we are discussing.

You could argue that the rat was addicted to the sexual stimulation it received; the rat chose to press the lever even when harmful consequences had begun to arise. Similarly, it's possible to find yourself conditioned to behaviors that result in your failure, just as the rat's pressing of the lever resulted in its death.

5.2.2 Classical Conditioning

The original and most famous example of classical conditioning involves the conditioning of Pavlov's dogs. During his research on the physiology of digestion, Pavlov noticed that, rather than simply salivating in the presence of food, the dogs began to salivate in the presence of the lab assistant who fed them. From this observation, he predicted that if a particular stimulus in the dog's surroundings were present when the dogs were presented with the food, this stimulus would become associated with food and cause the dogs to salivate.

In his initial experiment, Pavlov used a bell to call the dogs to their food and, after a few repetitions, the dogs started to salivate in response to the bell. Thus, a **neutral stimulus** (bell) became a *conditioned stimulus* as a result of repetitive pairing with the *unconditioned stimulus (food)*. Pavlov referred to this learned relationship as a conditional reflex. In modern psychology, it is referred to as a *conditioned response*.

Classical conditioning is a type of learning in which an organism comes to associate stimuli. A neutral stimulus (bell) becomes the *conditioned stimulus* that signals an *unconditioned stimulus* (food) and begins to produce a *conditioned response* (salivation) that anticipates and prepares for the unconditioned stimulus. This process is also called respondent conditioning.

Now that you understand simple conditioning, we are going to focus on the positive and negative consequences that conditioning can have in your life.

5.3 Conditioning Can Lead to a Failure Addiction

In section 2.2, you learned about inertia. In section 2.3, with the example of a widowed woman named Sally, you saw how inertia might act to trap a person in circumstances that do not allow her to maximize her success. Now consider the idea that a great deal of such counterproductive inertia occurs within, at the chemical level. The neurological biochemical model shows if no change in the production of the feel-good neurological peptides occurs in the hypothalamus, and if a continuation of production of the feel-bad neurological peptides occurs, the person continues to feel a negative mood. This, in turn, does not allow the person to seek other opportunities to feel good. The system comes to a grinding halt.

A person in a constant state of feeling bad day after day can be conditioned to feel bad. Externally, this may be expressed by various levels of depression and maladaptive behavior. You can actually become conditioned to producing bad or unproductive behavior. In a condition known as learned helplessness, to name just one example, humans have been shown to assume they have no control over their lives even when they do. If, for a while, their attempts to change their lives fail, they become blind to future opportunities, instead assuming that they have no choices in life. This has been shown to happen in other animals as well: in a canine study performed by psychologist Martin Seligman in 1967, a whopping two-thirds of his subjects displayed learned helplessness long after the circumstances preventing their progress had disappeared.[15]

In human studies on learned helplessness, one main factor separated the successful third from the other two-thirds: optimism. In other words, positive thoughts that focus on what you can personally achieve in your life will actually insulate you from becoming conditioned to fail.

In what ways are you currently conditioned to fail? In what ways have you learned to be helpless instead of taking charge of your own life? The most important part of all of this is that any and all operant conditioning effects, whether good or bad, are reversible, as long as the individual is able to gain insight into the situation and control the production of neurological peptides. Major changes can be within the individual's control. You can turn on all systems to emergency mode; start by doing things that make you feel good, regardless of what anyone might say or do. Pick two or three things you are going to intensely focus on that you know from previous experiences will make you feel great. Do not focus on anything else and devote 100 percent of your thinking and waking moments to achieving these goals. The more intense you are in the search, the faster you will notice the change within you.

There are no shortcuts: work hard and involve yourself with the things that make you feel good and you will feel better. This will turn on the creative and experimental part of you, to create new thoughts and new ideas.

5.4 Where is Your Personality?

In previous sections, it has become clear that your personality is a major factor affecting your ability to take advantage of the law of attraction and become conditioned toward success. In order to maximize your financial and personal potential, it can be helpful to learn more about the characteristics of personality.

A psychologist might say the personality is a complete set of behaviors to sum up the existence of the individual up to that particular moment.

A neuropsychologist might give the same definition, but add a set of behaviors creating emotional experiences formed through complex neurological biochemical reactions, which form billions of long- and short-term neurological connections in the brain to form the individual's personality and belief system.

Both answers are correct; the biochemical is much more complex but much easier to explain for our purposes.

In the neurological biochemical description, we refer to the personality as that area of the brain that has formed the neural net to include billions of neurological connections, with all of the life-building patterns and associations to people, places, things, and situations we experience on a second-by-second basis.

In other words, two different people can become conditioned toward very different behaviors, thus responding to any given situation in very different ways. If one student has experienced a strong mathematical background in school, and the other student has transferred in from a school that offered less mathematical training, they are going to approach their upcoming algebra test in very different ways. The first student, who is used to taking and excelling at such tests, will expect to succeed; the second student may fear failure based on other tests he or she has taken while settling in at the new school. This fear of failure may lead to negative thoughts that cause learned helplessness and prevent the second student from doing well on the test.

This process of forming associations that result in habitual behaviors starts from the moment of birth. A newborn starts life with two basic emotions, the feeling-good emotion, when the baby is not crying, and the feeling bad emotion, when the baby is crying.

Let's examine a simple explanation of this process. When a baby senses discomfort, a series of feeling-bad emotional peptide chains are produced and released into the bloodstream, causing the baby to cry. The moment the baby is pacified, the production reverses and a feeling-good emotional peptide chain is produced and released, causing the baby to stop crying. This is the start of the learning process. When the baby is hungry, the feeling-bad peptide chains is released and it cries; the moment you feed the baby, the feeling-good peptide chain is released and the baby stops crying. Because of this operant behavioral conditioning, the baby learns very fast—when it wants something it cries. This process of behavioral conditioning goes from very simple to extremely complex; those of you who have teenagers will be in total agreement. The baby's learning is the beginning stage of learning; from then on it grows exponentially to form the personality.

This building is all a process of neurological biochemical reactions with an ongoing series of complex combinations of chemical peptides that are produced in the chemical factory, the gland that sits in the middle of you brain called the hypothalamus. Every emotion you experience is formed through a complex peptide chain and then released into the bloodstream to be picked up by receptor sites in all of the cells in your body. It is the most magnificent chemical pharmacy in the universe.

5.5 The Key to Penetrating Your Belief System

As a part of each individual's personality, his or her belief system comprises billions of neurological long-term connections to form established patterns of the individual's reality. An individual is told "I saw a bird fly." The information is filtered through the belief system and processed as a true event. On the other hand, tell an individual, "I saw a cow fly," and the information is processed as false and passed to a different location for further processing to determine the validity of the information. The statement could be the beginning of a joke or the statement of someone delusional.

Every bit of information processed through your brain is filtered through this system. The process of creation works hand in hand with your belief system. Any information processed through your belief system as true continues for further processing. A five-story building is on fire, you are standing on the top floor, and you have to make a decision to jump or not. You look down and make an assessment—if there is an air bag, you jump. If you look down and there is no air bag, the information goes on for further processing. Do I have time to wait for a ladder? Or should I jump and take my chances on survival?

If I strongly believe I can make an extra $40,000 a year, the information goes on for further processing to the associative creative regions to find ways to manifest and convert it into reality. If I do not believe that it is possible, the thought goes right into the brain's recycling bin.

Let us look at this from a different perspective. Sexual excitement is an emotion we are all very familiar with. Visual cues come in through the visual cortex to the occipital lobe; information is processed and sent to other parts of the brain involving billions of connections in both hemispheres. The information is filtered through the internal personality-belief neurological biochemical net. From there, it passes for further processing in the personality system to the hypothalamus, which turns on the production of sexual feeling-good peptide chains in the bloodstream to target sexual cell receptors in the reproductive systems. It creates sexual behavioral arousal in both males and females. In the male, it causes an erection and in the female, clitoral erection plus lubrication. In the next step, information is filtered through the neurological belief system, which in turn leads to internal questions—Will this lead to a sexual encounter? Or is it going be to filled into the brain's recycle bin? This is where the situation becomes much more complex.

For example, a man is invited to a party and among the crowd is this month's *Playboy* centerfold. The internal question arises: *What are the chances of taking the centerfold home?* Depending on how he reacts to the situation, the outcome can go one of two ways.

Let's say this man was recently rejected by a different woman at another party. This negative experience could have conditioned him to failure. Now, in his learned helplessness, he takes the negative viewpoint that he has no chance with this beautiful woman—even though he has never met her before and has no way of knowing whether she will give him a chance. Instead of making an attempt to strike up a conversation with her, he hangs out silently by the punchbowl, letting an opportunity pass him by. Meanwhile, if he had made an effort to chat with the woman, he would at worst wind up no worse off than he had been—and he may have at least managed to learn something. In his learned helplessness, this man has trapped himself in his own reality.

Compare that to a more confident man who thinks positively about the future. He walks over to the beautiful woman and introduces himself. He looks her in the eye as he shakes her hand. He asks how she knows the hostess of the party, and one conversational topic leads to another. Does he take home her phone number? Maybe, maybe not. But one thing is certain: he has an astronomically better chance of success than the insecure, negative man lurking by the punchbowl.

Established patterns on the belief system will be evaluating the possibilities of a positive outcome. If at any time, the belief system stops the production of feel-good peptides, everything stops, very much like a car without fuel. Even though the sexual desires may continue, the man will disqualify himself because the negative aspect dictates, *This is not going to happen.* The defeating thoughts and low self-esteem will take over the production of more negative thoughts, leading to a negative outcome.

The personality belief net will continue to make situational assessments and negative internal negative statements such as: *She will never come home with me*; *She is too popular*; *She will pick somebody better than me*; and, worst of all, *What will I do if she comes home with me? Will I be able to perform?* or *Will I be able to satisfy her?* All of these internal statements producing negative thoughts create a negative outcome or performance anxiety.

What makes the personality patterns of a ten-year-old change so drastically as he grows older? The primary factor of change is the law of the attraction. It seems as we grow older, people that had encouraged us and told us, "Go ahead, it can be done," "You can be whatever you want to be" are the same people that later tell us, "Do not try that, it is too hard," or "It is not going to happen," or "You are not smart enough." They have good intentions, but are not aware they are conditioning the person to settle for less. It is most likely the same conditioning they experienced with their parents. It is as infectious as a viral flu.

If you change your belief system to be more positive, you will be ready to make the law of attraction work for you. Once your improved belief system prompts the continual creation of positive thoughts, it's only a matter of time before you reach your goals.

Surround yourself with mediocrity and you will be a part of the group. However, surround yourself with success and surprisingly, success comes your way. If you are in an unsuccessful environment for several years, you can easily be conditioned to that state of mind. You can sit in a dead-end situation for years unless you change your mentality.

A good example of an unsuccessful environment can often be found in an office setting. In some offices, the decor is drab, the air conditioner is over-productive, the boss is unreasonable, and every worker in the place has learned that it feels better to complain and get sympathy from one another than work to make the venture more successful—even though this ultimately harms their own individual careers. While everyone shivers under gusty vents in their gray cubicles, muttering complaints about how unfair it is that they are expected to finish a ten-page memo before quitting time, they miss opportunities to develop new skills, organize efforts to petition for the improvement of their office at the next board meeting, and form other strategies that might improve the situation.

Sure, the initial environment isn't these workers' fault. But their reaction to it is what sets them up for perpetual failure. Ironically, their distaste for their environment is the very thing that will trap them in it.

5.6 Addictions Aren't Just Psychological—They're Biochemical

We have biochemical needs and cravings, and we bring to ourselves situations that fulfill the biochemical needs of the cells of our body by creating situations that meet our chemical needs. When your body has an addiction, it will always need a little bit more in order to get the biochemical rush, so by definition, an individual losing control of this emotional state can become an addict. An addiction is an out-of-control emotion that you cannot stop.

So, can we say we are addicted to a person we love, or is it the anticipation of that emotion we are addicted to? The person is only the stimulus and the emotional need is the addiction, because we can fall out of love with that person and replace that person with another and the emotional-addiction situation remains the same. So it is not the person we are addicted to, but the emotional situation that is attached to the person.

The important point that most people need to understand is that emotional addictions are labeled psychological, but the underlying process is all biochemical. They come alive by the richness of our experiences, which intensify the biochemical production of the emotion and the display of an external psychological symptom. This external display of symptoms is the result of a highly complex neurological biochemical process.

The intensity of an addiction is dictated by the number of peptide chains released and the proportional increase in receptors on the targeted cells.

A sexual addiction and a heroin addiction use the same biochemical process and the same cell structural receptors. In reality, we can become addicted to any peptide chain or any emotion. Humans are always in constant search of emotions. Every thought that is created has an emotional aspect.

Thus, not every addiction has to result in negative outcomes. Some people are addicted to success—which simply leads to more success. This is an extreme example of the application of the law of attraction. While caution is important when you suspect you are addicted to success (after all, you don't want to work yourself into ill health), the mechanisms behind addiction can be used to benefit you.

5.7 Could You Have a Behavioral Addiction?

A behavioral addiction, by definition at the neurological biochemical level, can be created by a continuous thought of a desired behavior causing a repetitive, overwhelming, relentless pursuit of the desired result by the release of neurological biochemicals that can condition the need for the constant behavior. The conditioning strength of the behavioral addiction can range from mild to severe. The amount of neurological biochemicals released determines the severity of the conditioning. Most of the time, we think of a behavioral addiction as a negative event. An addiction to sex, even though we understand it as a pleasurable experience, can become pathological when the addiction leads to a criminal action such as rape, or to promiscuity, which could lead to other severe health consequences, such as AIDS.

Because we think of an addiction as negative or something that disturbs the stability of our behavior, we often have difficulty classifying a positive behavioral addiction or an addiction that can be beneficial, evoking a positive outcome. An addiction to success is a perfect example of what we are discussing. Success can be conditioned in the same manner as some of the addictions with the negative outcomes. An addiction to exercise is another positive addiction, reinforced by having a thinner, more fit body. Any behavior that is biochemically reinforced with a feeling-good peptide will be duplicated.

5.8 Could You Have a Substance Addiction?

A substance-abuse addiction can be just as devastating as one of the negative behavioral addictions, with one huge difference: substance abuse is much easier to condition than all of the others combined. The methods remain the same, but the stimulus is much easier to attain. A substance-abuse addiction, such as heroin addiction, works exactly in the same manner with the same pathways—brain structures releasing the same neurological biochemicals. Another, cocaine addiction, is just as powerful. The most common substance addiction is nicotine addition. Studies show a rise in nicotine in cigarettes of 10 percent in the past six years. Cigarette manufactures have to answer to their stockholders— so that addiction is a legal, multibillion dollar business causing a huge health risk worldwide. Another, caffeine addiction, is not as devastating as the others but try abruptly stopping drinking coffee if your body has been conditioned to drink several cups a day. Your hypothalamus is not going to be very kind to you.

5.9 How Would You Develop an Addiction to Heroin?

First you need the goal and the ultimate objective, which is to feel overwhelmingly great. In order to reach that state of feeling great, you will need a hypothalamus, and you can find one encased in the very center of your brain. You need to introduce the chemical into your blood system, preferably by injection. In this case, the substance is heroin. The chemical will travel through the blood system to the brain, where neurological biochemical reactions and pathways will evoke the constant release of peptide chains composed of amino acids that will act on millions of receptors in targeted cells that form the pleasure centers in the brain, causing such a strong craving for the chemical that a conditioning effect can happen after one single trial. After the effect wears out, the hypothalamus will begin the process of producing a peptide chain of the opposite effect, to cause discomfort and invoke very creative thoughts in order to find ways to repeat the first process. The need to continue the cycle can cause an individual to perform inconceivable acts to get that next fix. A chemically induced feeling-good peptide is the same as the thought-induced peptide, but the one that is chemically induced performs faster and has a more direct effect on the production of peptides. The difference is the speed of the production of the desired peptide chain. Experiencing such an overwhelmingly good feeling that you'd never before experienced causes the uncontrollable need to have it again. This is by definition an addiction.

5.10 How Would You Develop an Addiction to Success?

First you need the goal and the ultimate objective, which is to feel overwhelmingly great. In order to reach that state of feeling great, you will need a hypothalamus and you can find one encased in the very center of your brain. You need to create thoughts and ideas (pride, desire, gratitude, hope, empathy, happiness, euphoria, and joy) that influence the hypothalamus to produce constantly the same emotional feeling-good biochemical peptide chains composed of amino acids. The peptide chains will travel through the bloodstream to neuronal biochemical nets composed of billions of neuronal biochemical connections, and will act on billions of receptors in targeted cells that form the personality, belief system, and creative centers. The creative centers begin the process of manifestation of the thoughts and ideas. From the first small goal you set, addiction begins. Even if your goal is simply to contribute $25 a month to a retirement plan, every time you successfully meet that goal, the positive feelings you experience will increase your addiction to success. Soon, your goals will grow larger and more complex, but with every step toward a larger, overarching goal, you will experience emotional thoughts of accomplishment, causing the same identical procedure to occur and stimulate the hypothalamus to produce more of the same emotional feeling-good peptide chains. When this cycle becomes repetitive, the person is in a relentless pursuit of and constant search for the next successful project or idea. This, by definition, is an addiction.

Following the instructions in the next chapter will help you condition yourself toward beneficial behaviors. If you adhere to the instructions it offers, you will eventually become addicted to success.

5.11 Do Only the Things That Make You Feel Good

If you are able to pursue knowledge without any interference of your emotions, your body will experience huge changes in the ability to integrate new information, with less interference from judgmental filters or maladaptive behaviors created by previous emotional neural nets. The changes you create will establish new connections that will change your perception of what you can do, which then will become your new reality.

Success then becomes not one simple process of positive attracts positive or negative attracts negative. When you create a thought such as career goal and the thought has a long-term possibility of manifestation, the biochemical process always has to do course corrections. The objective is to keep producing the positive feelings (pride, desire, gratitude, hope, empathy, happiness, euphoria and joy) to maintain a constant production of emotional feeling-good peptide chains, which continues to shape and construct that long-term manifestation.

You can experience this learning when you start to perform your own experiments. Once you are ready, you can start practicing so you, too can benefit from the results. There is no greater learning experience than when you say, "It is true; I tried it and it works *(reinforcement)*."

CHAPTER 6
The Instructions

6.1 Can You Guess What the Last Chapter Is About?

I have briefly discussed quantum mechanics as one of the major contributions in twentieth-century physics. It is probably the closest science has come to a fundamental universal description of the underlying nature of how we experience reality. I've mentioned all of the concepts we have embraced that sound as bizarre as nuclear reactors and space shuttles would sound to an individual from a thousand years in the past—that go against all our intuition and common sense. It all sounds more like a science fiction than anything else because of the intangible nature of all of forces we cannot see.

I have also applied, explained and covered throughout the entire book basic principles in modern behavioral psychology and principles of conditioning in our society.

I have covered extensively basic principals in neuropsychology, neurological biochemistry, biochemical processes of addictions, biochemical processes of the placebo effect, the neurological biochemical processes of the creation of a thought, the neurological biochemical construction of your personality and the associative centers of your brain as they relate to the neurological sciences.

I have included government statistics clearly showing where the majority of the population is heading. I have demonstrated the basic root of the problem including deceptive ideas from the media and denial conditioning.

And most of all I have provided clear succinct solutions with explanations and methods to simple psychological and neurological chemical applications.

This last chapter is your instruction manual to create the critical major correctional shift everyone needs. Thoughts become things.

6.2 The Importance of Following Instructions

The secret key to creating major correctional changes in your life is well defined and explained in this final chapter. The information and knowledge you have read so far is from documented scientific contributions of several hundred years of research in advances in the fields of quantum mechanics, psychology, neuropsychology, and the neurological medical sciences. It will help you to improve your finances, achieve your goals with certainty, enjoy financial success, create happiness, improve your relationships, improve your health, and attain freedom and peace of mind.

This instructional manual will enable you to plan, manage, and control every aspect of your future. You will be able to address your specific financial needs and happiness. And with perseverance and practice, this can lead to the creation of multiple streams of income.

Planning for your financial future is a necessary condition for a successful lifestyle. And given the changing nature of our economic environment, it makes even more sense to take charge of your financial future with a greater sense of urgency.

Now is the time to change your conditioned mediocrity mentality and put your thoughts (pride, desire, gratitude, hope, empathy, happiness, euphoria, and joy) into action so that you are well prepared to meet the challenges that lie ahead. It is not wise to be at the mercy of external forces. We live in a society where the rich will get richer and the poor will get poorer. If things continue in the direction they are headed, the middle class will be facing extinction.

I am offering you proven methods and strategies to enable people just like you to achieve success in their financial objectives with confidence. Based on all of this in-depth, broad-based multi-disciplinary scientific knowledge and extensive research, I have distilled and packaged the secret key to create life-changing corrections using proven methods of psychological operant conditioning in the form of an operational instructional manual.

This operational manual is based on operant conditioning, and includes simple rules, action examples, and an instruction guide with step-by-step instructions to enable you to plan and achieve your goals.

Within minutes, you could be applying these valuable strategies to improve your life and finances. Successful people do not wait for things to happen—they make things happen. People do not plan to fail—they fail to plan.

People do not always follow instructions. If you purchase a desk today, it comes in a box, unassembled. This benefits both the manufacturer and the consumer, because the desk can be sold at a lower cost and the savings are passed on to the consumer. The problem is that when you take the desk home, you find a fifty-page instruction booklet. Consumer statistics show that the average person attempts to build the desk without reading the instructions, and as a consequence, the building process becomes an unpleasant experience. Not following the instructions often leads to not completing the project on the first attempt and this is my *warning to you.*

I am going to use the information you just read to warn you in the interest of saving you precious time. *You have to follow the instructions or you will not succeed in your first attempt.*

Are you ready to get started?

6.3 The Nine Steps of the Millionaire Mindset
These nine steps will all be described in detail:

1. Gather and store your materials

2. Start generating positive thoughts

3. Consider your goals

4. Determine your routes to success

5. Dismiss interference

6. Remind yourself that you have all the time in the world

7. Reread, reread, reread

8. Seize opportunities

9. Duplicate, duplicate, duplicate

6.3.1 Step 1: Gather and Store Your Materials

Your tools for conditioning yourself toward success are deceptively simple.

Action item: Purchase a notebook and a corkboard (or bulletin board of some kind). Find a safe place to keep your notebook, where not one person or family member can read it. This notebook is for your eyes only; you are not to share it or discuss the content with anyone.

Keeping the journal confidential keeps you out of harm's way from an unsolicited opinion, which causes interference and leads to the production of a different emotional type of peptide chain, which neutralizes the production of the one with the desired outcome. *Under any circumstance, are you going to share any of your thoughts, goals, ideas or plans with absolutely anyone?* Every thought, idea, or plan you create will be under your total internal conscious control. The moment you share any information with anyone, you will receive an opinion, and that opinion, whether good or bad, will neutralize your thoughts and give you interference. Interference is the major killer of dreams. Once injected, without fail, it will interfere with your creative process. In order to make an accurate assessment of your potential, anyone else would have to be in your shoes. It is a well-known fact that the individuals closest to you will create the most interference, and in many cases, are the primary causes of your failures. Picture this scenario: You attend an investment seminar and you are introduced to the foreign exchange currency trading market, where you can make 21 percent to 50 percent monthly on your investment. You come home to your spouse to discuss this amazing opportunity, and your spouse proceeds to tell you how crazy that sounds—it all sounds like it is not true. Who has ever heard of a company paying 21 percent to 50 percent monthly on your money? Your spouse has indirectly created an enormous amount of interference, and you forget the investment opportunity and continue putting your hard-earned money in your local bank's 2 percent-a-year certificates of deposit. This type of interference came from one of the persons closest to you and totally destroyed an opportunity that could have created a large amount of income, because there are reputable foreign exchange currency trading companies that can teach you how to learn these trading strategies and can make you these high percentage of profits on your investments. The only person in this world that knows your potential is you. *Keep your thoughts and goals to yourself.*

6.3.2 Step 2: Start Generating Positive Thoughts

The first proactive move you can make is to begin avoiding the common negative thoughts that could seriously jeopardize your future and the lifestyle you dream.

Infectious thoughts cause failure.

If you think about procrastination, you will procrastinate.

If you do not realize you will need a specific amount of money to sustain you each month, you won't make it.

If you think you can draw *full* Social Security benefits to survive, you won't.

If think you are not in good health, you won't be.

If you are not thinking to create a financial plan to survive, you won't create it.

If you are not creating a financial plan to retire, you won't retire.

If you have a false hope of retirement, you won't retire.

If you think about not succeeding, you won't succeed.

Stop focusing on these common negative thoughts and mistakes, and make sure you are not falling into the traps they can create. In contrast, consider these examples of proactive thoughts:

Any level of success I desire is within my reach.

Now is a great time to begin gearing my life toward success.

I have what it takes to accomplish my goals.

Action item: On the first page of your notebook, write down five positive thoughts that are specific to you—your dreams, your abilities, and your future. Take a moment to let these thoughts sink in. As you progress toward the end of this book and toward a complete understanding of the law of attraction, revisit that first page of your notebook now and again to ensure that those thoughts are continuing to help you harness the power of the law of attraction.

It is important to be constantly searching for proactive thoughts. You have to be open to ideas as they become available. Don't let the above exercise mark the beginning and end of your effort to create proactive thoughts; add to your list as you proceed through the material, and try to narrow your positive thoughts to a more and more specific plan of action as you go. A good starting place for such a plan of action is to consider what sort of career or business you would like to work toward.

6.3.3 Step 3: Consider Your Goals

Now that you have begun training your brain to think positively, it's time to start considering what your specific goals should be. How do you want to make your income? Try to keep an open mind as you consider ways to maximize your potential.

For example, it might be a good idea to consider including a home-based business among your possible options. While this approach places a lot of responsibility on the individual and therefore isn't for everyone, it is a popular option among many financially successful people at the moment for a reason. CNN reports that a new home-based business is started in the United States every eleven seconds. Why?

Well, because a new home-based business offers a low start-up investment compared to a brick and mortar, or franchise, business. There is low monthly overhead, and you can start part-time while still employed, and create time leverage, residual income, and tax benefits for yourself. Tax expert Sanford Botkin says that a home business can result in tax savings of $3,000 to $9,000 per year.

You can follow this trend; however, do proceed wisely. Make sure you do your research. You are looking for an income-generating system that allows you to build substantial supplemental income, passively—where you do not have to give up your life, or your spare time, to run it successfully.

While considering your goals, it's important to look at the personality and lifestyle aspects that a certain goal would require. For instance, in the case of starting a home business, it might be helpful to consider the following criteria:

Do you possess a skill, such as graphic design or medical transcription, that might lend itself toward a home-based business?

If you do not possess such a skill, are you willing to put in the time and effort to acquire that skill?

Are the equipment costs and other start-up costs something you could reasonably pay for or finance sometime in the foreseeable future?

Are you willing to educate yourself on marketing and spend time and money on networking and advertising?

Are you skilled at seeking out information you might need to equip yourself, whether over the Internet, in a phone book, or in a library?

Have you demonstrated the ability to work efficiently without supervision?

Do you have, or are you willing to obtain, a rudimentary knowledge of tax policies and accounting practices as they might apply to a small-business owner?

As you can see, many considerations apply to this decision. If, for instance, you are an inefficient worker, working a non-salaried job at home might add a lot of additional work hours to your day. Take a hard look at yourself and think about what would make you the happiest professionally. What work environment is ideal for you? What sort of positive thoughts can you create in that direction?

You may want to get involved in network marketing. Many highly successful individuals such as Donald Trump have stated that if they were to lose all of their income, they would restart by looking for a product every consumer uses and sell it in a network marketing program. You need to be careful with the many network-marketing schemes; the key to success in this type of business is the product. The product must be one that everyone needs to use. A good example was the computer. In the 1980s, laptops were the product of the times; by positioning themselves in the market, those involved in the manufacturing of laptops became financially wealthy.

Today, an industry trend that will create more millionaires than the trends of the last two decades is the industry of VoIP, or Voice over Internet Protocol. There are ways to become involved in this industry that will revolutionize the next decade. Positioning yourself in a situation where you are receiving residual income from sales of the new technology will allow you to enjoy your retirement free and to the fullest.[16] No matter what path you intend to take toward success, take the first step today by generating goals that, through the power of the law of attraction, will help you reach financial success.

Action item: In your notebook, list five goals you know can be attainable, giving each goal its own page and writing the goal at the top. Be specific.

Action item: In your notebook, list five goals you think might be unattainable—at least according to some people! Again, give each goal its own page, writing the goal at the top.

When you are writing these goals, it is critical that you describe each goal with precision and clarity. For example, about one year ago, I wrote that I wanted to be involved with a successful company and open up a successful business in this bad economy. I didn't write "make more money" or "start a business." Instead, I listed specific criteria and described my ideal business. In November of 2009, I became associated with one of the fastest-growing telecommunications companies in the country. The company is called 5linx, and they are in the VoIP (Voice over Internet Protocol) business. Microsoft made over two thousand millionaires and three billionaires overnight when the company became public; 5linx is poised to do the same or better. Had I not been specific, a close acquaintance of mine would not have realized I was interested in telecommunications. But because I had articulated that specific niche to myself in my notebook, I was able to later mention it to him, opening a world of opportunity.

The more information you write about your goal, the better and faster results you can achieve. This page becomes your blueprint (neutral stimulus) of how the thought will be fabricated in your mind. You will create the thoughts with the following feelings in mind—pride, desire, gratitude, hope, empathy, happiness, euphoria, and joy. Your thoughts will continue to build around your initial thought exactly as you wrote it. The more you rehearse and the more attention you direct to the goal, the better you will feel emotionally *(consequence).* The consequence is slowly building and shaping the goal unconsciously; this is the part where most people fail, because they are consciously trying to understand an unconscious process. In basic neurological biology, you are creating an abundance of that particular emotional peptide chain, which leads to higher motivational experiences producing a cortical response in the creative regions of your associative centers; a subconscious process is activated to manifest the thought or the goal into reality. Since the building process is unconscious, the results will always appear to you as a lucky opportunity or accident, when indeed the cortical regions have been working overtime, relentlessly pursuing it 24-7.

6.3.4 Step 4: Determine Your Routes to Success

Action item: On the back of each goal page, draw a line down the center. On the left-hand side, write at least ten different actions or methods that will help you achieve this goal. Be very creative, since you are the only one that will be reading this.

By writing your goals and strategies on a piece of paper (neutral stimulus) and listing the ways to manifest the thought, you are actually engraving the image in your mind. The actual construction of this image (consequence) originates from the production of an emotional neurological biochemical peptide chain of amino acids. The task for the unconscious associative creative regions is to find ways to manifest the thoughts.

6.3.5 Step 5: Dismiss Interference

Action item: On the right hand side of the back of each goal page, write "interference." Then leave it blank. Nothing will stop you from achieving this goal.

When you leave the right portion of the page blank or write down, "Nothing or anything is going to stop me from achieving this goal," you occupy the mind, keeping it from having to think any thoughts that might stop the creative process.

Avoiding interference takes a great deal of practice; the popular misconception is that this is about positive and negative thinking, but it is far from it. It is about positive thinking and no thinking. The moment you buy into the "I will have only positive thoughts and no negative thoughts," your associative regions have just opened up a Pandora's box and created interference. The moment you say, "I won't have negative thoughts," you have just started to produce the wrong type of emotional peptide chain. So you leave the right side of the paper blank; this does not allow any thought processes to interfere with the process you are trying to create.

If you think of a positive thought as going forward and a negative thought as going in reverse, your thought process could be just like the passenger-jet aircraft we are all familiar with: they can only go in one forward direction. They have no reverse. Your positive thought can only go forward without any other thoughts to make it go in reverse. As long as all the chemical production is going forward, the unconscious mind will find a way to manifest it.

6.3.6 Step 6: Remind Yourself That You Have All the Time in the World

Action item: Somewhere on each goal page, write, "Time available to complete each goal:" and then fill in the answer: "as much as it takes."

Time is a critical factor and your success in achieving your goals is all based on leaving each thought timeless. You will have all of the time in the world to achieve it, and you must not assign any time constraints to any thoughts. All thoughts and goals are to be open-ended. The moment you put a time limit to the production of a desired outcome, you produce interference.

Some thoughts or goals will manifest faster than others; the length of time your unconscious creative region takes to manifest the desired outcome is *not* under your conscious control. Results will seem to appear as accidental discoveries. This will happen every time without fail. I caution you not to be surprised. Unattainable goals frequently manifest before attainable goals.

6.3.7 Step 7: Reread, Reread, Reread

Action item: Reread your goal pages as often as you can. Repetitive reading is a key strategy if you intend to use the law of attraction to make your dreams a reality.

Repetitive reading of the goal produces an ongoing rehearsal and an ongoing production of beneficial neurological biochemical peptide chains, therefore causing a saturation effect needed for creating awareness in the creative associative regions.

6.3.8 Step 8: Seize Opportunities

Action item: Remain vigilant for opportunities that will further your progress toward your goals.

Action item: When you find a potential opportunity, such as an ad in the newspaper, cut it out and attach it to your visual board (your corkboard or bulletin board). Review the board daily, focusing your thoughts on how to best take advantage of these potential opportunities.

Even in these economically difficult times, financial opportunities are constantly flowing, and your relentless thoughts of making a higher income are fueling the creative processes in the associative regions. Once your mind finds something that fits your belief system, it will open the door to the creative processes and the manifestation will suddenly appear only to you. The key is to be open to the opportunity so that you take action the moment it appears. This opportunity will come in ways that will only make sense to you. The best example I can give you is if you think of everyone speaking their own specific language. The opportunities you are seeking will always be in your language only, and only you will be able to recognize them when they happen. The reason most of the times they may look as if they are by accident is because of your unconscious process. Once your thoughts are firmly in place, the brain works on the manifestation even when you are not awake. Once again, you cannot share any of this with anyone. If you were to share your thoughts with anyone, the information you receive can affect the opening of your creative door, and when the opportunity arrives, your mind will be totally closed to it. Whatever opinion anyone has injected you with will cause interference, neutralize the flow of the neurological chemical trying to make it happen, and another one bites the dust.

A person recently wrote to me after attending several seminars. She wanted to express an immense gratitude for the success she'd acquired in the application of the concepts and procedures. The first thing she listed in her notebook was getting a job that would pay $10,000 more than what she currently made. She expressed how she pursued the idea and the thoughts of making the higher salary constantly. Every day, she made brief notes in her notebook under that particular goal. The notes consisted of the things she needed to do on a daily basis to acquire the much-needed job. The emotional process involved the desire, hope, and joy, and neurologically, the hypothalamus produced the peptide chains involving these emotions. A constant production of the same peptide chains produced an emotional feeling-good state (operant conditioning). The reinforcement phase continued the behavior of writing the daily notes and the recurring thoughts of the job acquisition. She states that what happened next appeared to evolve by accident, but she was aware that it was not accident. She claimed that a friend invited her to go to a job fair, and that she had never attended this type of opportunity. She claims she went because she felt her friend needed to find a job. She discovered there a job that would pay her $22,000 more per year. She applied and was hired. She confessed to me that the only thing missing in her daily notes was to attend a job fair. At the unconscious level, she had been having constant thoughts of the things she would purchase and of all the financial freedom she would receive from the higher income.

The thought is you want to increase your income an extra $30,000 because you want to be able to afford a nicer home and a newer automobile. You visit home developers and auto dealers, get brochures of homes and automobiles you want, and post them on a visual board. A visual board is a simple corkboard. You write it in your notebook, read it, rehearse it daily, install the thoughts in your mind, and relentlessly pursue the outcome 24-7, even though you have no clue how you can install this corkboard in any place you can see daily, without inviting comment. If anyone should ask you about the board and the brochures, you could tell them it is your dream board. *You are not to share the thought* (making an extra $30,000) *with anyone.*

You think about it constantly, you go to sleep thinking about the home and the car, you see yourself in the home, you see yourself driving the car, you visit furniture stores and see the type furniture you're going to buy, you look at the home brochures, and you check out every room and plan how you are going to decorate it. All of this is creating a constant neurological biochemical reaction in your unconscious mind, like a tornado, and once it stops, your mind has found a way to achieve it.

6.3.9 Step 9: Duplicate, Duplicate, Duplicate

The last part of this process is the most important in operant conditioning— the reinforcement promotes the neurological biochemical duplication of this process in all phases of any written goals. The process will come full circle, and you will have accomplished total closure once you achieve your first goal. The emotional feeling created by the release of neurotransmitters directed to cortical pleasure centers will condition this complete process.

The good news is that once you begin achieving your goals, this step will happen by itself, and you will slowly become conditioned toward success.

Action item: Start small. The more you believe in your ability to create positive outcomes, the more effectively the law of attraction will work for you. To begin building your confidence, start with a small goal. Tomorrow morning, when you wake up, write down your expected positive outcome for the day in your notebook. Do you plan to get through your entire inbox at work? Do you intend to fit in a workout or a walk with the dog? Choose a small goal that you can accomplish in one day and detail it in your notebook. Whether your goal for the day is to offer a friend the advice he requested in an e-mail a few days ago, get your taxes done, or sign up for an intramural sports team, you'll find that writing it down and thinking about it will get you better results with less effort. Once you see for yourself how effective the law of attraction can be, you will quickly gain the confidence you need to move on to bigger and bigger goals.

6.4 How the Steps Worked for Me

Let me explained how my example manifested into reality. My desire and hope was to create a successful business in what we can all see is a bad economy. My mind was open to an opportunity I would normally have no interest in. My mind was open to the opportunity because of the abundance of chemicals unconsciously shaping and constantly searching for the opportunity. I was able to see the opportunity only because of my mental process, otherwise I may have passed on it. My reinforcement for my process is the fact that I was able to see the opportunity, and in the first sixty days, I made a substantial amount of profit and aggressively pursued 10,000 shares of the company, which are issued at given levels of success.

6.5 Ergomania

If I was asked to describe this book to anyone in a few words, I would say this book is about psychological financial healing.

The *ergomaniac* is the medical-legal term for a person addicted to work, better known as the typical **workaholic**. The word **"Ergomania"** itself is composed of *work* and *alcoholic*. The term was identified by psychologist Richard I. Evans, a professor of psychology at the University of Houston. The phrase is also attributed to psychologist Wayne Oates and his 1971 book, *Confessions of a Workaholic*. The term gained widespread use in the 1990s, as the result of a wave of the self-help movement centered on addictions, forming an analogy between harmful social behaviors, such as overwork, and alcohol addiction.

A workaholic in the negative sense is characterized by popular side effects such as neglect of family and friends, stress, and in severe cases, work-related obsessive- compulsive disorder.

It is necessary to warn you throughout the process of operant conditioning described in this last chapter that you can very easily become an ergomaniac. Ergomania is considered a behavioral addiction and the phrase implies the individual continuously driven to acquire whatever particular *reinforcement* the *stimulus and consequence* is providing. The reinforcing end product of the process causes the addictive condition: Even in cases where the work is not enjoyable, the individual is driven by the reinforcement.

Addictions usually have a negative connotation, and the term *workaholic* imposes a negative label even though it could be recognized as a positive personality trait and is often used by individuals expressing their devotion to their work in a positive manner. History shows the majority of the greatest contributions to science were by individuals with obsessive-compulsive personality. Shakespeare, Newton, Dalton, Beethoven, Einstein, Lincoln, Heisenberg, Bohr—all had obsessive-compulsive personality traits, so if you become overly successful you are not in bad company.

The work is the *neutral stimulus* usually associated with a specific *goal*. The process of shaping and creating is the *consequence*, and the achievement or the manifestation of the goal is the *reinforcement*. Multiply the process one hundredfold and you have success by default, and you are on your way out of the 98 percent group. It is also very important to be aware when this process is developing. This will allow you to provide a balance between success and the amount of work you are devoting to the process of becoming successful. The reinforcement of the process is extremely powerful and it will continue to shape and create (*consequence*) more success. If it happens without a conscious internal monitoring, the neuro-biochemical process accelerates, and this is where the individual can get into a situational addiction to the process. Even though this can create a positive financial situation, the quality of life is affected tremendously because the work becomes the sole purpose in the life of the individual. In order to be totally successful in life, you must have a balance between work and the quality of family life.

In other cases, the *workaholic* is not associated with financial *reinforcement*, but could be pursuing success (reinforcement) in sports, music, and art. It is important to note the brain does not recognize the difference between a *substance addiction* and a *behavioral addiction*. They both use the same neurological biochemicals and follow the same neurological pathways. *Operant conditioning* is the gatekeeper for the addiction process, and as harmless as the instructions in this chapter may seem to you, they can and will create an *addiction to success*.

6.6 A Final Word

This book teaches you that the power to become successful is all within you. As you can plainly read, if you follow basic rules of behavioral modification, you can apply the process to every facet of your life. A fair warning to all of you, as you may already know, is that nothing in life comes easily. Behavioral conditioning is a gradual process and the only process that can produce significant changes in your life. The information you have learned is extremely powerful, and in order to create the changes, you must follow the steps without question. There are no shortcuts; if you follow the process and instructions, you will create any and all changes you need to create financial changes or any other goals you desire.

Now that you have important behavioral-modification, Psychology 101 knowledge, I want you to pay close attention to your environment and surroundings. We are constantly bombarded everywhere we go with the sale of something. It could be anything from a product to a political idea (*stimulus*). They are all trying to get you to purchase the product and use it, or if it is an idea, buy into it (*consequence*). Once you buy the product or buy into the idea, it becomes their reinforcement. And if the product or the idea made you feel good, it becomes your reinforcement, and the process will repeat over and over until you are not reinforced any longer, or something betters comes along and reverses the first conditioning to start the second conditioning.

Most of you will begin immediately after reading this book, and without fail, you will noticeably become aware of the changes taking place within you. The neuro-biochemical internal emotional changes will produce a feeling-good or joyful state of desire for achievement of goals, hope to improve financial conditions, a sense of accomplishment by slowly shaping and creating (consequence) your thoughts and manifesting them into reality, and a deep sense of gratitude that you are the architect of unleashing this power within you. You may not have known you had it, and it is now the center of your creative process.

If you do not feel any of these changes, you are doing something wrong. If this is the case, you are not applying or understanding the material. Go back and read the book as many times as it takes to learn the material. A conditioning pattern will begin to emerge by the time you achieve your first six goals, especially if getting the hell out of the 98 percent group is your reinforcer. Money is one of the strongest psychological reinforcers on the planet. If you do not believe me, visit Las Vegas.

The neurological biochemical process of operant conditioning described in this last chapter is the production of one exclusive peptide chain of amino acids created by thoughts that gives you the feeling-good emotions (pride, desire, gratitude, hope, empathy, happiness, euphoria, and joy). This feeling-good emotion in abundance fuels the creative associative regions of your personality. The creative regions work at an unconscious level and are constantly shaping and constructing the thought to manifest the thoughts or goals into reality. A change of emotion causes a change in the peptide chain. For example, if you are pursuing a desired change in career and you are constantly focused on attaining this goal, there is a constant, specific neurological peptide chain in production that will continue to be in production as long as there is an ongoing emotional desire. If you start to produce thoughts that involve not being able to achieve the goal because of xyz (interference), your brain has just changed into a different type of production of a different neuro-peptide chain that will neutralize the production of the original peptide chain involved in your first goal and leave you in a state of noticeable dissatisfaction. Let's say you have a feeling of happiness because you are accomplishing a goal, and all of the sudden, a different, negative thought is generated. The production of the second, negative, emotional peptide chain will cause interference of the first and neutralize it to the point that if the negative thought continues, it will take over the production and remove the feeling-good situation with a feeling-bad condition. It then becomes a numbers game, saturation of a different emotional peptide neutralizes the first one *(interference)* and creativity stops.

Once you become conditioned to obtaining desired results, you are constantly producing an abundance of neurotransmitters in the pleasure regions, and this could lead to noticeable side effects. Slow periods can cause a decrease of the emotional feeling good neurological chemicals produce. This response is identical in nature of that of an addict beginning to experience withdrawal symptoms. Other peptide chains are fabricated and the individual begins to feel stress and anxiety. This condition can worsen and cause a work-related obsessive-compulsive personality disorder.

We have covered an enormous amount of scientific and psychological information with one main focus in mind. My main contribution to you is to convey all of this information in simple terms, so that you are able to duplicate all of these behavioral modification strategies and apply them to your everyday life.

The main key to your success involves your mindset. This entire book has been dedicated to modifying your mindset. This is the mindset of every successful entrepreneur. I am sure by now you are aware that without this blueprint, you are just part of the group conditioned to failure. This mindset is all under the conditioning process we have discussed. It is time to put the book down and follow the steps carefully. This process will not happen overnight; it is an ongoing process, and because it is a gradual change, it can take several months. The main objective is to stay focused and understand the process of interference. The process will never fail you if you are perseverant and relentless in attaining your goals. The key to your success is all in this book. I have been told by several individuals who have read this manuscript that every time they read it they discover something they missed in their previous reading. I recommend you read this book several times, and if you know of anyone that is in need of a financial change, make them aware of this information. I want to end this with an invitation to all of you who create the changes and achieve your goals because of the information I have provided you. Please write me with your accomplishments, and if you allow me, I will publish your results in the next book I will be writing—*The Cure for Financial Cancer.*

The outstanding public debt as of September, 2009 is: *$11,817,386,190,787.* The estimated population of the United States is *306,951,470,* so each citizen's share of this debt is *$38,499.11.* The National Debt has continued to increase an average of *$3.89 billion per day* since September 2, 2007.

It is virtually impossible to begin to understand the huge financial crisis each and every citizen is facing. It does not take a financial genius to recognize this country is bankrupt. Yet everything continues from day to day and business as usual. The average American is conditioned for failure. Those conditioned to succeed (2 percent) will succeed, and those conditioned to fail (98%) will undoubtedly fail. *The rich will get richer and the poor will get poorer.* The bankruptcy rate is the highest it has ever been. The rate of individuals' losing their homes is at its highest level. The second wave of foreclosures, of individuals not able to pay for their home taxes, is just around the corner.

With only 1 percent of individual tax returns being audited, 16 percent of people simply do not their taxes, and one out of six individuals do not pay taxes at all. Will even more people stop paying? The average American household makes just enough to cover bills, and a large of percentage of the populations expects refunds from their tax returns.

Do not be fooled by the media and politics; *the rich will get richer and the poor will get poorer.* Take the latest presidential popular topic of taxes. Both presidential candidates in the 2008 election, Barack Obama and John McCain, targeted this important topic to get elected. I admired both candidates for their idealistic designs to resolve this financial crisis, but if you have been sold on the idea that individuals in the 2 percent group are going to pay higher taxes and bail out the economy, you need to pull out your calculator and do the math. Let me shed some light on this huge misconception. The great majority of the 98 percent group does their taxes with available inexpensive software like TurboTax or Tax Act. Some use firms like H&R Block, and some use inexpensive accountants. The fact you have been sold that the rich are in a higher tax bracket is all an illusion. You are probably not aware of the tax-avoidance techniques available to the higher tax bracket individuals. Yes, there is a huge difference between tax avoidance and tax evasion. The average person making more than $250,000 a year has tax-avoidance high-end lawyers and high-end accounting firms do his or her taxes. They have expensive purchased-asset-protection programs, including blind Nevada and Delaware corporations and offshore accounts to protect them legally from other individuals—and the government. Let us think about this. At this moment, the money in your bank is protected by the Federal Deposit Insurance FDIC up to $250,000, and in January of 2014, it goes down to $100,000. What that means is that if you have one million dollars in a U.S .bank and the bank fails, you can sit back and wait to receive $100,000 from a bankrupt government. On the other hand, most offshore accounts are guaranteed by Lloyds of London for a total of twenty-five million dollars. So you tell me where would you place your hard-earned money.

In theory, the rich should be in the higher tax brackets, but in reality, the good majority are in the single digits. Those fortunate to be in the 30 percent or higher group are learning fast to legally keep as much money as possible in their portfolios.

The reason is quite obvious. If you belong to the 98 percent group, it is time to bail out. Time is critical; you have the instruction manual in front of you. Start today—save yourself, and follow the yellow money brick road.

Glossary[17]

Associative regions. The extensive outer layer of gray matter of the cerebral hemispheres largely responsible for higher brain functions, including sensation, voluntary muscle movement, thought, reasoning, and memory.

Autonomous response. A response generated by the part of the vertebrate nervous system that regulates involuntary action, as of the intestines, heart, and glands, and that is divided into the sympathetic nervous system and the parasympathetic nervous system.

Bankruptcy. A legal proceeding in U.S. Federal Court entered into by borrowers who are unable to pay their debts. In Chapter 13 bankruptcy, the borrower files a payment plan with the court and promises to make partial payments to creditors.

Biochemistry. The study of the chemical processes in living organisms. It deals with the structure and function of cellular components such as proteins, carbohydrates, lipids, nucleic acids and other biomolecules.

Blueprint. Something intended as a guide for making something else; "a blueprint for a house."

Classical conditioning. A basic form of learning in which a neutral event (unconditioned stimulus) initially incapable of evoking certain responses acquires the ability to do so through repeated pairing with other stimuli that are able to elicit such responses.

Conditioned beliefs. Beliefs based on available information. This idea is formalized in probability theory by conditioning. Conditional probabilities, conditional expectations, and conditional distributions are treated on three levels: discrete probabilities, probability density functions, and measured theory.

Consequence. A part of behavioral operant conditioning and the process of pairing a neutral stimulus with the result *(consequence)* to achieve reinforcement.

Copious. Great in quantity or number, profuse, abundant; having an abundant supply.

Delusion. A fixed, false belief that is fanciful or derived from deception.

Entrepreneur. An individual who organizes a business venture and assumes the risk for it.

Ergomania. An obsession developed through operant conditioning. An obsessive drive to achieve financial success or success not related to any type of financial gain.

Foreclosure. The legal proceedings initiated by a creditor to repossess the collateral for the loan that is in default.

Galactic phenomena. An unusual event relating to a galaxy (especially our galaxy the Milky Way); "the occurrence of an event in the galactic plane."

Hallucinations. In the broadest sense, a perception in the absence of a stimulus. In a stricter sense, hallucinations are defined as perceptions in a conscious and awake state in the absence of external stimuli, which have qualities of real perception.

Holographic pattern. A technique that allows the light scattered from an object to be recorded and later reconstructed so that it appears as if the object is in the same position relative to the recording medium as it was when recorded. The image changes as the position and orientation of the viewing system changes in exactly the same way as if the object were still present, thus making the recorded image (hologram) appear three dimensional.

Hypothalamus. The gland responsible for certain metabolic processes and other activities of the Autonomic Nervous System. It synthesizes and secretes hormones, often called hypothalamic-releasing hormones, and these in turn stimulate or inhibit the secretion of pituitary hormones. The hypothalamus controls body temperature, hunger, thirst, fatigue, and circadian cycles.

Karma. An Eastern religious concept in contradistinction to "faith" espoused by Abrahamic religions (Judaism, Christianity, and Islam), which view all human dramas as the will of God as opposed to present—and past—life actions. In Eastern beliefs, the karmic effects of all deeds are viewed as actively shaping past, present, and future experiences. The results or "fruits" of actions are called *karma-phala*.

Law of attraction. The notion that positive thoughts attract positive outcomes. Interpretations of New Thought thinkers is that the Law of Attraction says your thoughts (both conscious and unconscious) dictate the reality of your lives, whether or not you are aware of it. Essentially "if you really create a thought and truly believe it is possible, you will attain it," and if you focus on negative aspects of the thought you are creating, it will most likely not become reality.

Mediocrity. Averageness, commonness, commonplaceness, normality.

Metaphysicians. Investigators of the principles of reality transcending those of any particular science. Cosmology and ontology are traditional branches of metaphysics. It is concerned with explaining the fundamental nature of being and the world. Someone who studies metaphysics would be called either a "metaphysician" or a "metaphysicist."

Molecular biology. The study of biology at a molecular level. The field overlaps with other areas of biology and chemistry, particularly genetics and biochemistry. Molecular biology chiefly concerns itself with understanding the interactions between the various systems of a cell, including the interactions between DNA, RNA, and protein biosynthesis as well as learning how these interactions are regulated.

National Debt. Government debt (also known as public debt or national debt) is money (or credit) owed by any level of government; either central government, federal government, municipal government, or local government.

Neuropsychology. The basic scientific discipline that studies the structure and function of the brain related to specific psychological processes and overt behaviors. The term neuropsychology has been applied to lesion studies in humans and animals. It has also been applied to efforts to record electrical activity from individual cells (or groups of cells) in higher primates (including some studies of human patients). It is scientific in its approach and shares an information processing view of the mind with cognitive psychology and cognitive science. It is one of the more eclectic of the psychological disciplines, overlapping at times with areas such as neuroscience, philosophy (particularly philosophy of mind), neurology, psychiatry, and computer science (particularly by making use of artificial neural networks). In practice, neuropsychologists tend to work in academia (involved in basic or clinical research), clinical settings (involved in assessing or treating patients with neuropsychological problems—see clinical neuropsychology), forensic settings (often assessing people for legal reasons or court cases or working with offenders, or appearing in court as expert witness) or industry (often as consultants where neuropsychological knowledge is applied to product design or in the management of pharmaceutical clinical-trials research for drugs that might have a potential impact on CNS functioning).

Neurotransmitters. Endogenous chemicals which relay, amplify, and modulate signals between a neuron and another cell. Neurotransmitters are packaged into synaptic vesicles that cluster beneath the membrane on the pre-synaptic side of a synapse, and are released into the synaptic cleft, where they bind to receptors in the membrane on the postsynaptic side of the synapse. Release of neurotransmitters usually follows arrival of an action potential at the synapse, but may follow graded electrical potentials. Low level "baseline" release also occurs without electrical stimulation.

Neutral stimulus. A stimulus which initially produces no specific response other than focusing attention. In classical conditioning, when used together with an unconditioned stimulus, the neutral stimulus becomes a conditioned stimulus.

Operant conditioning. The use of consequences to modify the occurrence and form of behavior. Operant conditioning is distinguished from classical conditioning (also called respondent conditioning, or Pavlovian conditioning) in that operant conditioning deals with the modification of "voluntary behavior," or operant behavior. Operant behavior "operates" on the environment and is maintained by its consequences, while classical conditioning deals with the conditioning of respondent behaviors, which are elicited by antecedent conditions. Behaviors conditioned via a classical conditioning procedure are not maintained by consequences.

Peptides amino acids. Short polymers formed from the linking, in a defined order, of α-amino acids. The link between one amino acid residue and the next is called an amide bond or a peptide bond. Proteins are polypeptide molecules (or consist of multiple polypeptide subunits). The distinction is that peptides are short and polypeptides/proteins are long. There are several different conventions to determine these, all of which have caveats and nuances.

Quantum mechanics. A discipline explaining the behavior of matter and energy on the minute scale of atoms and subatomic particles. The study reveals how particles can have wave-like properties and waves can have particle-like properties.

Reinforcement. In operant conditioning, reinforcement occurs when an event following a response causes an increase in the probability of that response occurring in the future. Response strength can be assessed by measures such as the frequency with which the response is made (for example, a pigeon may peck a key more times in the session), or the speed with which it is made (for example, a rat may run a maze faster). The environment change contingent upon the response is called a reinforcer.

Supernatural. Not existing in nature or subject to explanation according to natural laws; not physical or material; supernatural forces and occurrences.

Theologians. The study of God, deriving from the Greek word *theos*, meaning "God," and the suffix *-ology* from the Greek word *logos* meaning (in this context) "discourse," "theory," or "reasoning." Augustine of Hippo defined the Latin equivalent, *theologia*, as "reasoning or discussion concerning the Deity." Richard Hooker defined "theology" in English as "the science of things divine." More generally, it is the study of religious faith, practice, and experience, or of spirituality. Theologians use various forms of analysis and argument (philosophical, ethnographic, historical, spiritual, and others) to help understand, explain, test, critique, defend, or promote any of myriad religious topics.

Theory of relativity. The theory of relativity, or simply relativity, generally refers specifically to two theories of Albert Einstein: special relativity and general relativity. However, the word "relativity" is sometimes used in reference to Galilean invariance.

Theosophical. A system of belief based on mystical insight into the nature of God and the soul.

Transfer factor. Immune messenger molecules found in all higher animals. They are found in white blood cells, colostrum, and eggs. They are often given credit for the perpetuation of species by transferring immunity against many pathogens that would otherwise kill the offspring. Transfer factors can be found in humans and animals like cow.

Visual cortex. The part of the brain that is responsible for processing visual stimuli.

Selected Bibliography

Amaral, Julio Rocha do and Renata M.E. Sabattini. "Placebo Effect: The Power of the Sugar Pill," Cerebromente. http://www.cerebromente.org.br/n09/mente/placebo1_i.htm

Assaraf, John. *Having It All: Achieving Your Life's Goals and Dreams*. Hillsboro, OR: Atria, 2007.

Aven, Anisa. "The Secret Law of Attraction—How to Make it Work." *Creative Manifesting*. http://www.creatavision.com

"Basic Concepts and Laws of Chemistry." *Informika*. http://schoolsector.relarn.ru/nsm/chemistry/Enu/Data/

Bellis, Mary. "Thomas Edison: Edison's Early Life," About.com. http://inventors.about.com/od/estartinventors/a/Edison_Bio.htm

"A Biographical Sketch of Bill Harris," *Centerpointe Research Institute*. http://www.centerpointe.com/about/bills_bio.php

The Biochemical Aspects of Addiction—L. Ron Hubbard and the Narconon® drug. http://www.heroinaddiction.com.

Byrne, Rhonda. *The Secret*.Hillsboro, OR: Atria, 2006.

"Cathy Goodman Willed Cancer Out of Her Body Using the Secret." Ezine Articles: 263,670 Expert Authors Sharing Their Best EzineArticles. http://ezinearticles.com/?Cathy-Goodman-Willed-Cancer.

Cloninger, C. Robert. *Theories of Personality: Understanding* Persons, 5th ed., New York: Prentice Hall, 2007.

Diamond, Marie. "Feng Shui with Marie Diamond." *Learning Strategies*. http://www.learningstrategies.com/FengShui/Home.asp

Dispenza, Joseph. *Evolve Your Brain: The Science of Changing Your Mind*. Deerfield, FL: HCI, 2008.

Dow, Marty. "Abundance—Understanding the Cosmic Law of Attraction," *LCSW*. http://www.law-of-attraction-info.com/visual.htm.

Doyle, Bob. "Introduction to the Law of Attraction and Unlimited Wealth," *Self Growth*. http://www.selfgrowth.com/articles/Doyle12.html.

Dwoskin, Hale and Jack Canfield. *The Sedona Method: Your Key to Lasting Happiness, Success, Peace, and Emotional Well-being*. Sedona, AZ: Sedona Press, 2003.

Einstein, Albert—Biography. *Nobel Prize Web Site*. http://nobelprize.org/nobel_prizes/physics/laureates/1921/einstein-bio.html

Emoto, Masaru. *Water Secrets Revealed: Discover the Miraculous Messages from Water*. Life Enthusiast.

http://www.life-enthusiast.com/twilight/research_emoto.htm

Giardunio, Karen. "Dr. Ben Johnson Cured Himself—Using The Healing Codes and the Secret of Lou Gehrig's Disease," *Article Alley*, 13 July 2007. http://www.articlealley.com/article_186099_22.html

"Good Vibrations and the Law of Attraction: What a Magnetic Combination," *Law of Attraction Info*. http:// www.law-of-attraction-info.com/vibes. html

Goswami, Amit. *Official site and blog of Dr. Amit Goswami, PhD—Quantum Physicist*. http://www.amitgoswami.org

"Gratitude," *Steve Pavlina.com: Personal Development for Smart People*. http://www.stevepavlina.com/blog/2007/01/gratitude/

"The Greatest Manifestation Principle in the World," Web site. http://www.greatestmanifestationprinciple.com/

Hameroff, Stuart and Roger Penrose. "Quantum Consciousness," *Toward a Science of Consciousness: The First Tucson Discussions and Debates*, eds. Hameroff and Kaszniak. Boston: MIT Press, 1997.

Hicks, Abraham. "Money and the Law of Attraction Cards," Abraham Hicks. Publications. http://www.abraham-hickslawofattraction.com/lawofattractionstore/product/CRD-MLOA.html

"Hypothalamus Function—A Comprehensive Overview," *Wellsphere*. http://www.wellsphere.com/wellpage/hypothalamus-function

"Interview with Bob Proctor," *The Larry King Show*, CNN, 8 May 2008.

"Isaac Newton Biography," St. Andrews, Scotland: University of St. Andrews. http://www-history.mcs.st-andrews.ac.uk/Biographies/Newton.html

"Jack Canfield Interview—The Law of Attraction," *Oprah Winfrey Show*, 8 February 2007.

"Joe Vitale—Star of the Hit Movie, *The Secret*." http://www.joevitalesecret. com.

"John Dalton," *Biographybase*. http://www.biographybase.com/biography/ Dalton_John.html

Lang, Susan. "Dopamine Linked to a Personality Trait and Happiness," *Cornell Chronicle*, 24 October 1996. http://www.news.cornell.edu/ Chronicle/96/10.24.96/dopamine.html

"Lincoln, Abraham—Biography," Official White House Web Site. http:// www.whitehouse.gov/about/presidents/AbrahamLincoln.

"Ludwig von Beethoven," *8notes.com*. http://8notes.com/biographies/ beethoven.asp

McFarlane, Thomas J. "Quantum Mechanics and Reality," Integral Science. www.integralscience.org/sacredscience/SS_quantum.htm

"Mike Dooley—Star of the Hit Movie, *The Secret*." http://www. mikedooleysecret.com.

Monti, Daniel and Anthony Bazzan. *The Great Life Makeover.*New York: Morrow, 2008.

Niemi, Maj-Britt. "Placebo Effect: A Cure in the Mind," *Scientific American*, February 2009.

"Operant Conditioning vs. Classical Conditioning," Dog Manners, http:// www.dogmanners.com/conditioning.html

Pert, Candace B., PhD. Blog. http://www.candacepert.com/blog/blog.htm.

"Plato," *Britannica Philosophy Pages*. http://www.philosophypages.com/ph/ plat.htm.

"Population and Household Economic Topics," U.S. Census. http://www. census.gov/population/

Proctor, Bob. *Is the Law of Attraction Hype? Bob Proctor Explains*, DVD, 2009.

Ray, James Arthur. "Create Harmonic Wealth in All Areas of Your Life." Web site. http://www.jamesray.com

"Rhonda Byrne Interview—The Law of Attraction," *Oprah Winfrey Show*, 3 May 2006.

"Shakespeare: William Shakespeare Biography," Enotes. http://www.enotes. com/william-shakespeare/shakespeare-biography.

Sroka, Krzysztof. "Gratitude and the Law of Attraction," *Ezine Articles: 263,670 Expert Authors Sharing Their Best EzineArticles*. http://ezinearticles. com/?gratitude_and_the_law_of_attraction

"Tax Statistics," Statistics of Income Division, IRS, 2009. http://www.irs.gov/ taxstats/index.html

U.S. National Debt Clock: Real Time. http:// www.usdebtclock.org

"Use the Law of Attraction to Attract Money." *Attract Anything! Attraction in Action.* http://www.attractanything.com.

Uzan, Jean-Phillippe and Benedicte Leclerq. *The Natural Laws of the Universe.* New York: Springer, 2008.

"Wage by Area and Occupation," U.S. Bureau of Labor Statistics, 6 December 2007 htttp://www.bls.gov/bls/blswage.htm.

"What percentage of the U.S. population makes more that $250,000?" Annenberg Political Fact Check, 20 April 2008. http://www.factcheck. org/askfactcheck/what_percentage_of_the_us_population_

Endnotes

1. Jean Sahadi, "Recession Hits Social Security Hard." CNNMoney, http://money.cnn.com/2009/05/12/news/economy/SocSec_Medicare_trustees_report/index.htm

2. Greenspan Commission, "Report of the National Committee on Social Security Reform," January 1983. Social Security Online. http://www.ssa.gov/history/reports/gspan.html

3. Peter J. Ferrara, "The Comping Financial Collapse of Social Security, "The Freeman Ideas on Liberty. http://www.thefreemanonline.org/featured/the-coming-financial-collapse-of -social-security/

4. U.S. Debt Clock, http://www.usdebtclock.org/, accessed 14 April 2010.

5. "Super Bowl Ad: E*Trade 'Wasted $2 Million Bucks, 1999" *YouTube.* http://www.youtube.com/watch?v=BnQMq5wtZcg, accessed 21 March 2010.

6. *Wikipedia.org.* http::/www.en.wikipedia.org wiki/ - cite_note-2

7. Thomas J. McFarlane, "Quantum Mechanics and Reality," *Integral Science,* 1995. http://www.integralscience.org/sacredscience/SS_quantum.html

8. Ibid.

9. "Why Lottery Winners Lose it All," *Lendingtree,* http://www.wealthisknocking.com/Why-Lottery-Winners-Lose-it-All.html.

10. John P. Hussman, PhD. "Weekly Market Comment,"14 February 2010. http://www.hussmanfunds.com/wmc/wmc100208.htm

11. Omar Hossini, "Are We Really Printing Money to Finance Our Debts?" *History News Network*, 26 January 2009

12. Erica Goode, "Power of Positive Thinking May Have Health Benefit, Study Says," *New York Times*, 2 September 2003.

13. Sharon Begley, "The Depressing News about Antidepressants," *Newsweek*, 8 February 2010.

14. "Transfer factor," *Physician's Desk Reference*, 2009.

15. "Learned Helplessness," *Wikipedia*. http://en.wikipedia.org/wiki/Learned_helplessness.

16. John Rapp,"Has Residual Income Become Our Generation's Retirement Plan?" 14 December 2009. http://www.associatedcontent.com/article/2478686/

17. All definitions taken from *Wikipedia*, http://www/wikipedia.org.